# INSIGHT PO[C...]
# SLOVENIA

D1458212

C153947727

KENT LIBRARIES
AND ARCHIVES

C 153947727

| Askews | |
| --- | --- |
| | |
| | |

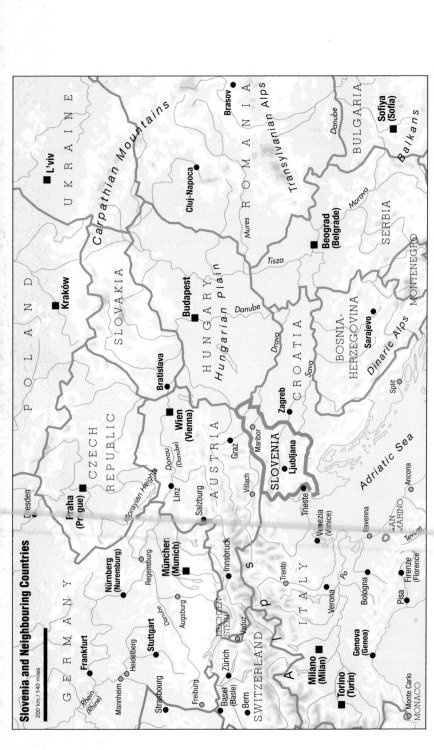

## Slovenia and Neighbouring Countries

*introduction*

# *Welcome*

This is one of more than 100 itinerary-based *Pocket Guides* produced by the editors of Insight Guides, whose books have set the standard for visual travel guides since 1970. With top-quality photography and authoritative recommendations, this guidebook aims to help visitors get the most out of the country during a short stay. Since establishing its independence in 1991 Slovenia has become a popular tourist destination, and in these pages, Insight Guides' expert on Slovenia, Jane Foster, has devised a range of itineraries to bring you the best of this small but fascinating country. Twelve full-day tours combine all the essential sights in the cities and the countryside, suggest overnight stays where a longer visit might be appropriate, and point you in the direction of companies that will help organise outdoor activities. The tours are grouped in four main areas: Ljubljana, Lake Bled and the Northwest, the Southwest and the Coast, and Maribor and the East.

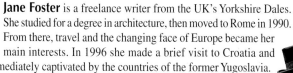

**Jane Foster** is a freelance writer from the UK's Yorkshire Dales. She studied for a degree in architecture, then moved to Rome in 1990. From there, travel and the changing face of Europe became her main interests. In 1996 she made a brief visit to Croatia and was immediately captivated by the countries of the former Yugoslavia. She decided to make Split, on the Dalmatian coast, her base and spent the next six years travelling extensively through Croatia, Slovenia, Bosnia Herzegovina, Serbia and Montenegro. She now lives in Athens, from where she writes for European and American travel publications, focusing on the Balkans.

# 6     **contents**

**Pages 2–3:** the beautiful backdrop of the rugged Julian Alps

## MARIBOR AND THE EAST

## LEISURE ACTIVITIES

## CALENDAR OF EVENTS

## PRACTICAL INFORMATION

## MAPS

## CREDITS AND INDEX

**Pages 8–9:** café life in Ljubljana

ZEMLJOVID

SLOVENSKE DEŽELI

IN POKRAJIN

IZDELAL IN NA SVITLO DAL

PETER KOZLER

1853.

# *History* *&Culture*

S lovenia entered the European Union (EU) on 1 May 2004 as one of 10 new members, a move seen by many as an historic milestone in the reunification of Eastern and Western Europe, which have been divided by political ideals for over half a century. However, many foreigners know little about the country (former US President, George W. Bush, in a much-publicised gaffe, confused it with Slovakia) so its past, as well as its location, needs some explanation. With Italy to the west, Austria to the north, Hungary to the east and Croatia to the east and south, this tiny nation has changed size, shape and affiliation many times through the ages.

In ancient times, the territory was inhabited by Illyrian tribes, who arrived from the south, and by Celtic tribes, who migrated from France, Germany and the Czech lands. The region's earliest known artwork is a 5th-century BC bronze urn, commonly referred to as the Vače situla. Found in Vače, near Litija, northeast of Ljubljana, it is now on display in the capital's Narodni muzej (National Museum). Created during the Iron Age, it is decorated with three bands of embossed figures: one portraying a solemn parade of men, horses and carts; one of priests and priestesses; and the third with sacred animals.

In the 2nd century BC, the Romans, who had already established the colony of Aquileia in northeast Italy, began advancing eastwards into Slovenia. The Julian Alps, in the northwest of the country, are said to have been named after the Roman Emperor Julius Caesar following his visit to the region in the 1st century BC. By the 1st century AD, the Romans had conquered the Illyrians and Celts, and founded the inland urban centres of Emona (Ljubljana), Poetovio (Ptuj) and Celeia (Celje). In the mid-5th century, Attila the Hun invaded Italy via Slovenia, attacking all the main Roman settlements on the way, and driving the Roman populace to build fortified towns along the coast and on nearby islands such as Capris (Koper) and Piranum (Piran).

## The First Slovenian State

The Slavs arrived in the 6th century, probably migrating from the area north of the Carpathian Mountains. A peaceful people with a classless society, they settled along the banks of the rivers Sava, Drava and Mura, close to lakes or in forests. They lived in close contact with nature, raising cattle and farming by the slash-and-burn method. They were superstitious and had many pagan gods. Under pressure from the Avars, they dispersed across the Balkans, east as far as the shores of the Black Sea and south along the Adriatic coast.

**Left:** *Map of the Slovenian Lands,* first published in 1853
**Right:** Habsburg Maria Theresa was a force for good in Slovenia

In the 7th century, the Slavs founded the first Slovenian state, Karantania, but as of 748 they came under Germanic rule, first under the Frankish Empire of the Carolingians and then under the Dukes of Bavaria. Under the Carolingians the Slavs began converting to Christianity, and around the year 1000 religious documents known as the Freising Manuscripts (in Latin script) were written, marking the first known records in the Slovenian language.

## Habsburg Domination

The Habsburgs took inland Slovenia in 1335, dividing it into the crown lands of Carinthia, Carniola and Styria. They remained in power until 1918, during which time the upper classes were largely Germanised and the Slovenian language and culture suppressed. Only the peasants, who organised determined but unsuccessful uprisings, clung to their Slavic identity.

During the late 16th century, the Protestant Reformation saw the publication of Primo Trubar's *Katekizem (Catechism)* in 1550 and the first Slovenian translation of the Bible in 1584, giving rise to an increase in literacy and raising the status of the Slovenian language. However, under Archduke Ferdinand, a Counter-Reformation took place in the early 17th century, reinforcing the Catholic faith and condemning Protestantism. In the meantime, the coastal towns had requested Venetian protection and remained under Venice until the fall of the empire in 1797.

To complicate matters further, a third foreign power, the Ottoman Turks, terrorised the entire Balkan peninsula during the 15th and 16th centuries. Repeated attempts to defeat Austria failed, but towns, castles and monasteries throughout Slovenia were heavily fortified to protect against possible attack and hefty taxes were imposed to fund defence projects. The situation improved slightly during the 18th century when Empress Maria Theresa (ruled 1740–80), one of the few Habsburg rulers who did anything positive for the region, introduced compulsory primary school education (in German). Her son Joseph II (ruled 1780–90) continued in a similar vein, abolishing serfdom in 1782 and encouraging religious tolerance. This period also saw the building of the first public cultural institutions such as theatres and libraries, and the first Slovenian-language newspaper, *Lublanske Novize (Ljubljana News)*, founded by the poet and journalist Valentin Vodnik in 1797.

Habsburg domination was interrupted from 1809–13, when Slovenia became part of Napoleon's short-lived Illyrian Provinces. At the time, it was believed that all South Slavs were of Illyrian descent, hence the name. The region stretched from Graz in Austria all the way down the east Adriatic to include Dalmatia, and Ljubljana was chosen as its capital. This was a period of liberation and national awakening, as the French introduced the use of the Slovenian language in schools and administration. The period was well regarded by Slovenian intellectuals, and also inspired the idea of a south Slav union, bringing together Slovenes, Croats and Serbs.

**Left:** 19th-century engraving: Napoleon bestows the Legion of Honour

*history/culture*

When Napoleon's French Empire collapsed, Slovenia returned to Habsburg rule. They reintroduced the feudal system, but the Slovenian spirit had been awakened. This was best reflected in the writing of France Prešeren (1800–49), author of *Zdravljica (A Toast)*, which became the national anthem in 1991.

During the Central European Revolutions of 1848, Slovenian intellectuals founded the Zedinjena Slovenija (United Slovenia) movement, calling for the unity of all Slovenian lands and full recognition of the Slovenian language. Although unsuccessful, the movement laid down the path for future generations. In neighbouring Croatia, Bishop Josip Strossmayer was preaching the idea of south Slav unity, in which Serbs, Croats and Slovenes would live in one nation. He, too, was ahead of his time.

On the economic front, the mid-19th century saw the dawn of the railways, with lines running from Trieste to Vienna and Budapest passing through Ljubljana and Maribor, and these improved communications gave rise to increasing industrialisation. Nonetheless, due to poverty, the late 19th century was to see mass emigration, primarily to the USA.

## World War I and the Rise of Communism

In 1914, the assassination of the Austrian Archduke Franz Ferdinand in Sarajevo led Austro-Hungary to declare war on Serbia. The Triple Entente (Russia, France and Britain) took the side of the Serbs, and promised part of Slovenia to Italy if it would join forces against Austria and Germany. The Italians began advancing east into Austro-Hungarian territory, forming a front line along the River Soča. Many Slovenes, although eager to liberate themselves from Habsburg domination, fought against Italy in an attempt to keep their country intact.

The Austro-Hungarian Empire finally ended in 1918. Inland Slovenia became part of the newly-formed Kingdom of Serbs, Croats and Slovenes (renamed the Kingdom of Yugoslavia – Land of Southern Slavs – in 1929), while the 1920 Treaty of Rapallo awarded the coast to Italy. At the same time communism was on the rise. The Communist Party of Yugoslavia was founded in 1919; in 1937 Josip Broz Tito (1892–1980) became its leader, and in the same year the Communist Party of Slovenia was born.

## World War II

In 1941, Hitler declared war on Yugoslavia, and the Axis forces occupied the country. Tito set up the anti-fascist Partizan movement, which was joined by Slovenia's Osvobodilne fronte (Liberation Front), founded by the

**Above:** the Archduke Franz Ferdinand, not long before his assassination

Communist Party of Slovenia along with other left-wing intellectuals. When the war ended in 1945, Slovenia became one of six republics of the Socialist Federal Republic of Yugoslavia, with Tito installed as president.

Despite the end of hostilities, parts of the northwest Adriatic coast remained disputed territory. The situation was resolved in 1954, when the so-called Zone A (including Trieste) was awarded to Italy and Zone B (Istria) was divided between Slovenia and Croatia.

## Tito's Yugoslavia

Half-Slovene, half-Croat by birth, Tito proved a charismatic and astute leader. In 1948 he broke with Stalin and the USSR, but managed to remain on reasonable terms with both the communist East and the capitalist West during the Cold War, cleverly gaining favours from each side. Yugoslavia kept a market economy based on workers' self-management (co-operatives); Yugoslavs were free to travel abroad and foreigners could enter the country without visas. In 1956, Tito, along with presidents Gamal Abd al-Nasser of Egypt and Jawaharial (Pandit) Nehru of India, founded the Non-Aligned Nations, an association of countries that declined to align themselves with either of the two world superpowers, the USA and the USSR.

In the 1960s, the country saw a period of rapid industrialisation and an impressive rise in the standard of living, but as the economy grew, so did the gap between the richer and poorer republics. Slovenia and Croatia began to resent paying taxes to Belgrade to subsidise poorer regions. Tito's motto, *Bratstvo i Jedinstvo* (Brotherhood and Unity), was the key to holding Yugoslavia together and quelling nationalist aspirations. Minority groups (in the case of Slovenia, Italians along the coast and Hungarians in the northeast) were granted an impressive degree of cultural freedom, and had their own schools, cultural clubs, TV and radio. In 1974 Tito introduced a new constitution-giving the individual republics more independence, a move that Serbia's Slobodan Milošović would later try to reverse.

Tito died in Ljubljana in 1980, having held power for 35 years. His funeral was attended by representatives of 127 countries from across the political spectrum. Aware of the imminent problems that would face Yugoslavia after his death, he left behind a rotating presidency, so that each republic would take the helm for one year, thus trying to prevent any one of them becoming too dominant. The system was doomed to failure.

## The Slovenian Spring

During the 1980s, economic crisis set in throughout Yugoslavia. By now, tiny Slovenia, accounting for only 8 percent of the nation's population, was pro-

**Above:** Marshal Tito in 1946

ducing a quarter of Yugoslavia's hard currency exports but the profits were under Belgrade's central control and Slovenes became increasingly frustrated.

Although Slovenes had always been considered hard-working and conservative, during this period Ljubljana became Yugoslavia's centre of alternative culture. The city saw a flowering of pressure groups rallying for causes ranging from ecology to gay rights. Laibach (a group of avant-garde musicians and ideologists), together with IRWIN (a group of painters), founded NSK (an art collective of musicians, painters, actors and designers). The liberal weekly *Mladina*, originally set up as a communist youth magazine in 1943, was becoming increasingly daring in its attacks on political and military issues. In 1988, three of the magazine's journalists and one army officer were arrested and put on trial by the Yugoslav National Army (JNA) Military Council. The JNA ruled that the magazine was counter-revolutionary and that it was linked to a foreign-backed conspiracy to overthrow the regime. This trial was the catalyst for the founding of an organised Slovenian opposition movement, which led to the so-called Slovenian Spring and Slovenia's secession from Yugoslavia.

Meanwhile, in Serbia Slobodan Milošović had come to power, and with him came a rise in Serbian nationalism. In the summer of 1988, he abruptly ended the autonomy of Kosovo, following a series of riots by ethnic Albanians, who made up 90 percent of the population in the province. Slovenes, along with their Croatian neighbours, began to worry that Belgrade's leadership was going one step too far, and that they might come under Milošović's thumb.

To add further complications, the fall of the Berlin Wall in 1989 marked the breakdown of communism throughout the Eastern Bloc. Thus Yugoslavia was no longer so important to US strategic interests – indeed, it seemed the West was eager to see the demise of the last remaining European communist state (apart from Albania).

## The End of Yugoslavia

In Belgrade in January 1990, at the Fourteenth Congress of the Yugoslav Communist Party, Slovenian delegates made an unprecedented move by walking out of the assembly, having been angered by the Serbian and Montenegrin delegations' rejections of every single proposal they put forward. The event was to signal the beginning of the end of Yugoslavia.

In April 1990, multi-party elections were held in Slovenia and a non-communist government formed, bringing with it calls for autonomy with the threat of secession. In December 1990, the republic held a referendum in which 88 percent of the electorate voted for independence. Belgrade, predictably, rejected the Slovenia's request to secede.

On 25 June 1991, Slovenia (along with neighbouring Croatia) declared independence. The following day, the JNA began moving towards the Slovenian

**Above:** the avant-garde band Laibach was part of the 1980s protest movement

border, where it was met by territorial defence units that had begun importing and stockpiling arms at the same time as the JNA had been trying to remove them from the country. Fortunately, as there were no territorial claims and the population was made up almost exclusively of Slovenes (unlike in Croatia, where Serbs formed a substantial group), Milošević let Slovenia go and the JNA pulled out (moving south into Croatia) after the so-called Ten-Day War.

On 15 January 1992, Slovenia was recognised by the European Union and the US, and in May of the same year it was admitted to the United Nations.

## Independence

Since gaining independence, the centre-left Liberal Democrats have dominated Slovenian politics. The priority issue during the 1990s was joining the EU, although one of the stumbling blocks was disputed property rights – Italy claimed that Italians who had fled after World War II were the legal owners of houses they had abandoned. Meanwhile, the economy was experiencing a

difficult period, as the region had been thrown into chaos by war. Slovenia had lost its natural trading partners (other former-Yugoslav republics), gained an influx of refugees, and tourism was at an all time low.

In 1998 Slovenia put forward its EU application. On 23 March 2003, a referendum was held in which 89.6 percent of the electorate voted in favour of Slovenia entering the EU and 66 percent opted for NATO membership.

### Slovenia Today

In 2004, Slovenia achieved two long-term goals: on 29 March it became a member of NATO, and on 1 May it joined the EU. By this time, with a GDP per capita income of US$12,000 a year, Slovenes were earning twice as much as the accession country average and 70 percent of the EU average. Of the five countries left from what was once Yugoslavia, Slovenia was exporting more than all of the others put together, and that with a population of only 2 million compared to former Yugoslavia's total 22 million.

However, the blot on the country's copy book is the case of the *izbrisanji* (erased), some 18,000 people from other republics of former Yugoslavia who found themselves living in a new country when Slovenia claimed independence, but never made successful applications for Slovenian passports. Their names were erased from the national register, leaving them stateless, and a referendum held in 2004 saw their hopes of gaining residency and other rights annulled.

On a happier note, the economy is booming. On 1 January 2007, Slovenia became the first of the new EU member countries to adopt the euro. By 2008, Slovenia had a GDP per capita of some, €22,500 a year, putting it on about the level of Greece.

**Above:** celebrating Slovenian independence

## HISTORY HIGHLIGHTS

**1st century BC** Romans arrive, conquer local Illyrian and Celtic population. Build villas along coast and found inland urban centres of Emona (Ljubljana), Poetovio (Ptuj) and Celeia (Celje).

**6th century AD** Slavs arrive in region.

**7th century** Founding of Slavic Duchy of Karantania, the first Slovenian state, stretching from Lake Balaton in present-day Hungary to the Adriatic Sea.

**8th century** Region comes under control of Franks. Slovenes begin converting to Christianity.

**9th century** Dukes of Bavaria assume control of region.

**1000** Compilation of Freising Manuscripts, the first known record of written Slovenian.

**13th century** Coastal towns come under Venetian protectorate, lasting almost 500 years. Capodistria (Koper) becomes main administrative centre of Venetian Istria.

**1335** Habsburgs take inland Slovenia, dividing it into Austrian crown lands of Carinthia, Carniola and Styria.

**15th and 16th centuries** Ottoman Turks cause havoc throughout Balkans, making repeated attacks on region. Follows a succession of unsuccessful peasant uprisings.

**1580s** Protestant Reformation brings first Slovenian translation of Bible.

**17th century** Counter-reformation reintroduces Catholicism.

**1797** Demise of Venetian Empire. Coastal towns pass to Habsburgs.

**1809** Slovenia becomes part of Napoleon's Illyrian Provinces, with Ljubljana as capital. For first time, Slovenian becomes official language in schools and administration.

**1814** Fall of Napoleon. Slovenia returns to Habsburg control.

**1914** Assassination of Archduke Franz Ferdinand in Sarajevo sparks outbreak of World War I.

**1918** The demise of Austria-Hungary. Inland Slovenia becomes part of the Kingdom of Serbs, Croats and Slovenes, while the coast goes to Italy.

**1941** Hitler declares war on Yugoslavia. Slovenia occupied by Axis forces. Tito founds anti-fascist Partizan movement.

**1945** Tito founds Federal Democratic People's Republic of Yugoslavia, with Slovenia as one of six constituent republics. Under his leadership minority groups are granted a large degree of cultural freedom.

**1974** New constitution gives greater autonomy to individual republics and makes provision for secession.

**1980** Tito dies. Yugoslavia is left with system of rotating presidency.

**1980s** Economic crisis sets in. Slovenia and Croatia object to funding poorer republics. Milošević assumes power in Belgrade as Serbian nationalism grows.

**1989** Fall of Berlin Wall marks breakdown of Eastern Bloc and demise of communism in Europe.

**1990** A multi-party system is introduced in Yugoslavia and a non-communist government is elected.

**1991** Slovenia proclaims independence on the same day as neighbouring Croatia. Slovenia's relatively minor Ten-day War ensues before Belgrade decides to let Slovenia go.

**1992** EU and UN recognise Slovenia.

**1993** Membership of International Monetary Fund and World Bank.

**1998** Slovenia puts forward its EU application.

**2003** In a March referendum an overwhelming majority votes in favour of joining the EU and NATO.

**2004** Slovenia becomes a member of NATO, and is one of 10 new countries to join the EU.

**2007** Slovenia adopts the euro.

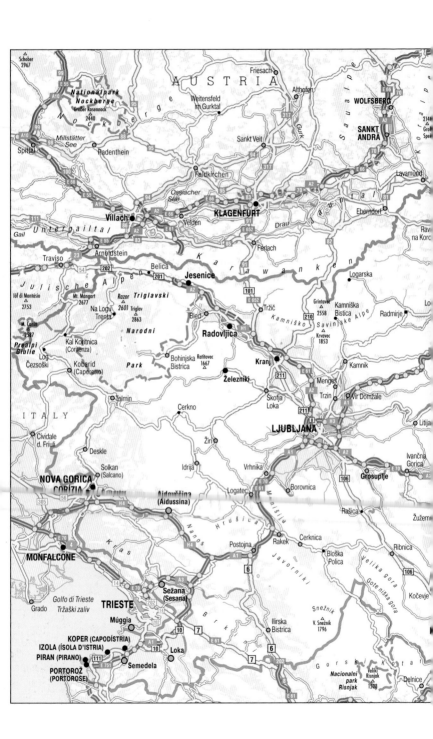

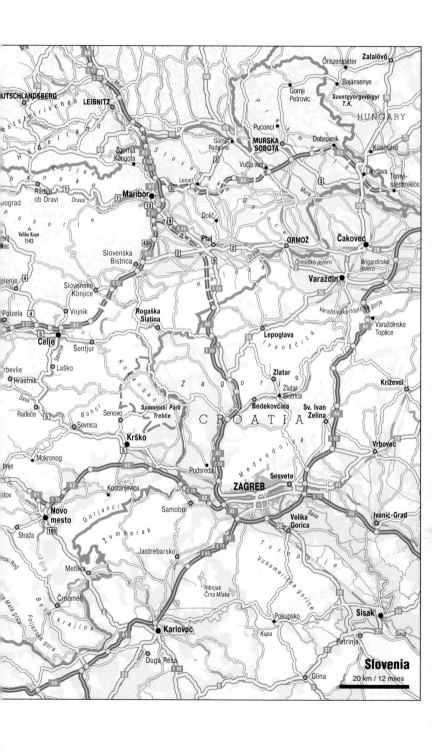

# *Orientation*

S lovenia is a small country – similar in size to Wales or Israel – but it encompasses great variations in landscape in relatively short distances. For instance, you can travel from the Adriatic coastline to the snow-capped peaks of the Julian Alps in just one day, and along the way you will pass carefully tended vineyards, thundering rivers, lush pastures and stunning mountain lakes.

The itineraries in this book cover four principle areas, beginning with the capital city, Ljubljana and the nearby Krka Valley, which is famed for its isolated monasteries. Then we move northwest to the popular lake-side resort of Bled, from where you can branch out to visit lovely Lake Bohinj and the Triglav National Park, then Kobarid and the Soča Valley. Piran, on the coast, is our next destination and the base for trips to the former mining town of Idrija, now better known for its lace-making, the casino town of Nova Gorica, the castles and caves of the Karst region and the Italianate port of Koper. Slovenia's second city, Maribor, in the east, is the final base, and your gateway to the wine region around Ptuj and the spa town of Rogaška Slatina.

## Getting Around

If you want to see it all, you will need at least two weeks – more to do the country proper justice – but if your time is limited, you can pick and choose and still see a lot of different aspects of Slovenia. Of course, it is eas-ier and quicker to get around if you bring or hire a car, but the country's comprehensive public transport network offers a reasonable alternative – trains and buses are plentiful and relatively inex-pensive. From Ljubljana's bus and railway stations, routes fan out to all the major towns, where local bus services take over to connect you with most of the surrounding villages. There are only a few remote regions (such as the Soča Valley) that would be difficult to reach without private transport.

Slovenia is a most interesting country, full of reminders of its long and involved history as well as evidence of its thriving modern economy and 21st-century outlook. It is a place where you can sit on a terrace on a balmy summer evening, sipping a glass of good local wine and drinking in idyllic views, or hurtle down world-class ski slopes in winter, hike in the mountains by day or stay out all night at one of the many coastal casinos that never close.

**Left:** the roofs of Ljubljana
**Right:** figure on a Stari trg façade

# Ljubljana

## 1. LJUBLJANA, CAPITAL CITY *(see map, page 24)*

**A full day in Ljubljana, exploring the baroque old town with its open-air market and cathedral, presided over by an imposing hilltop castle. Stroll along the riverside promenade, then spend the afternoon visiting the museums.**

*The first itinerary involves a considerable amount of walking, so comfortable shoes are essential. You should bear in mind that museums are closed on Monday but generally open until 6pm on other days.*

If you come to Slovenia by plane, Ljubljana will be your point of arrival. The city centre, like practically everywhere else in this country, is clean and well kept. Its two main elements are the river, lined with weeping willows and open-air cafés, and the stone castle, commanding fine views from its hilltop vantage point. Ljubljana has an easy-going, open-minded, youthful feel, largely due to the 50,000 university and college students who make up 15 percent of the total population of 330,000. During the 1980s, while still part of Yugoslavia, it established itself as the Socialist Republic's centre of underground culture, nurturing punk rock bands, performance artists and satirical magazines. The alternative streak lives on, complementing and often working in conjunction with the high-brow classical music and theatre scene, most notably during the summer festival *(see page 80)*, when open-air performances take place throughout the city each evening. The old town, with its cobbled streets, baroque façades, small art galleries, antiques shops and boutiques, can be explored comfortably on foot.

### City Squares and Bridges

Begin at the city's favourite meeting point, on the steps leading up to the pink-and-cream façade of the 17th-century baroque **Frančiškanska cerkev** (Franciscan Church) on **Prešernov trg** (Prešeren Square). The square itself is overlooked by an early 20th-century bronze monument to its namesake, France Prešeren (1800–49), who was Slovenia's best known poet and author of the national anthem. Inside the church, the high altar is the work of Italian sculptor Francesco Robba (1698–1757; *see also page 25*). To the right of the church, **Miklošičeva** runs directly north to the railway sta-

**Above:** outdoor café on the river bank. **Above Right:** the Grand Hotel Union
**Right:** the Tromostovje (Triple Bridge)

tion, and is lined with Secessionist buildings erected after an 1895 earthquake, the best known being the white **Grand Hotel Union** (see *Accommodation, page 92*) dating from 1905. Secessionist is another name for the Art Nouveau or, in German, *Jugendstil* architectural style that flourished around the turn of the century.

Two more fine examples of this style overlook Prešeren Square – the **Centromerkur** department store and the **Hauptmanova hiša** (Hauptman House). To the left of the square, **Trubarjeva** is lined with cafés overlooking the river. The **Café Bar Promenade** is a recommended spot for morning coffee. Not only is the coffee extremely good, but there is a fine view from the terrace of the castle rising behind the cathedral dome.

Leave Prešeren trg via the white **Tromostovje** (Triple Bridge), crossing the **River Ljubljanica** to arrive in the Old Town. The Tromostovje was originally a single bridge, built in 1842, and the two side bridges, with their graceful arches, were added in 1931 by Jože Plečnik (1872–1957), the architect responsible for many of the city's most beautiful 20th-century buildings. Born in Ljubljana, Plečnik studied under the renowned modernist Otto Wagner in Vienna, then moved to Prague, where he lectured at the School of Arts and Crafts and masterminded the renovation of Prague Castle, before returning to his native city in 1921.

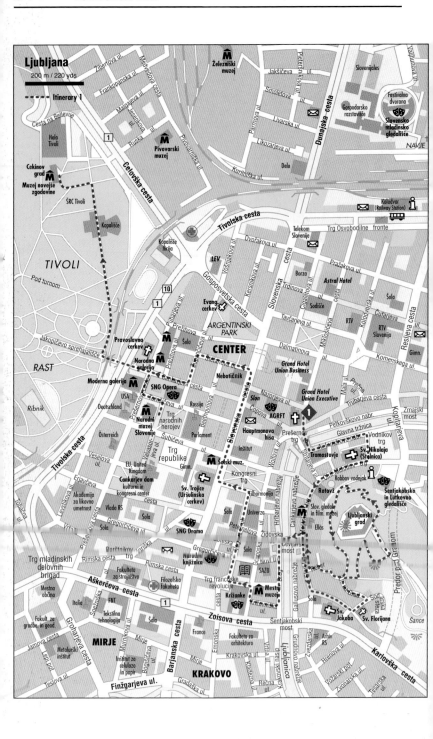

## Across the River

Once across the river, to your right lies the waterside promenade of **Cankar- jevo nabrežje**, lined with weeping willows and open-air cafés, including **Zlata ribica** (see *Eating Out, page 73*), a possible lunch stop. Each Sunday morning the promenade hosts a colourful and entertaining **antiques market** (8am–1pm). To the left of the Triple Bridge lies the **Glavna tržnica** (Central Market) designed by Plečnik in 1939. A classical, open-sided colonnade overlooking the river and running in a soft curve from the Triple Bridge to the Zmajski most *(see below)*, it hosts the fish market, butchers' stalls and bakeries. Note the stone spiral steps leading down to **Ribca** (see *Eating Out, page 73*), another good spot for lunch. Behind the Central Market, **Vodnikov trg** (Vodnik Square), watched over by a bronze statue of the poet Valentin Vodnik, is home to the open-air fruit and vegetable market (Mon–Sat 7am– 3pm). On the edge of the marketplace, the baroque **Stolna cerkev svetega Nikolaja** (Cathedral of St Nicholas) was built to plans by Andrea Pozzo, a renowned architect and Jesuit monk from Rome, in 1708. The bronze doors were added in 1996 to commemorate the visit of Pope John Paul II – the side door portrays the history of the Ljubljana diocese, while the main door celebrates 1,250 years of Christianity in Slovenia.

## Dragon Bridge and the Robba Fountain

Walk the length of Vodnik Square to check out the **Zmajski most** (Dragon Bridge), another fine example of Secessionist architecture, and one of the first concrete-and-iron structures in Europe, built in 1901 to mark the 40th jubilee of the Austro-Hungarian Emperor, Franz Josef. Each of the bridge's four corners is crowned with a fearsome winged dragon – local myth has it that they wag their tails when a virgin passes over the bridge.

From here retrace your steps across the marketplace, then turn left away from the river, then right, to arrive on **Mestni trg** (Town Square). The most notable building on this cobbled square is the 18th-century **Rotovž** (Town Hall), which stands slightly to one side of the highly-acclaimed **Robbov vodnjak** (Robba Fountain), designed by Francesco Robba in 1751 and apparently inspired by Bernini's Fountain of Four Rivers on Piazza Navona in Rome. The rivers depicted here are the Ljubljanica, the Sava and the Krka, with a unique

**Above:** sampling the delights of the Central Market
**Left:** the baroque Robba Fountain

three-sided obelisk supported by a dynamic mass of baroque sculpture. Also on the square, **Movia** *(see Nightlife, page 77)* is a sophisticated wine bar that's ideal for an evening aperitif.

Town Square leads into **Stari trg** (Old Square), more a narrow street than a square, which is lined with baroque townhouses accommodating boutiques, bars and cafés. This in turn flows into the medieval **Gornji trg** (Upper Square), home to **Špajza** *(see Eating Out, page 73)*, a highly regarded restaurant to which you may like to return for dinner.

### Ljubljana Castle

Follow Upper Square up as far as the 17th-century **Cerkev svetega Florijana** (Church of St Florian) then turn left into the side street of **Ulica na grad**, walking up as far as No 11, where you should take a narrow signed path through the woods to arrive at **Ljubljanski grad** (Ljubljana Castle; summer daily 9am–10pm, winter 10am–9pm).

Perched on a 376-m (1,233-ft) hilltop and surrounded by horse-chestnut trees, the castle as you see it today dates from the early 16th century, although there has been a fortress of some kind here for much longer. Down through the ages, it has been occupied by provincial rulers, becoming a garrison, then a prison. During a 1980s renovation by local architects, who were influenced by the Italian Carlo Scarpa, modern details in glass, steel and concrete were added. Today it is used for concerts and cultural events, including performances during the Ljubljana Festival. The ramparts shelter a café with tables in the courtyard – a perfect place to stop for a cold drink.

Visit the **Belvedere Tower** (Razgledni stolp) for great views as far as the Julian Alps. Below the tower, the **Virtual Museum** (Virtualni muzej; summer daily 9am–9pm, winter 10am–6pm; admission fee) portrays Ljubljana's 2,000-year history through a multimedia presentation, for which you wear special glasses for a 3D-experience and headphones with simultaneous translation in several languages, including English. The 20-minute shows run every 30 minutes, on the hour and the half-hour. Before leaving the castle, check out the Gothic Chapel of St George, decorated with frescoes from 1747.

Descend from the castle via the narrow path to the left of the main entrance, bringing you,

**Above:** Chapel of St George in the castle
**Left:** the Belvedere Tower

via **Studentovska**, back down to the riverside promenade. Take the pedestrian **Čevljarski most** (Shoemakers' Bridge), crossing the river to **Novi trg** (New Square). The original bridge, built of wood, was lined with cobblers' huts (hence the name), but what you see now was designed by the prolific Plečnik in 1931.

Walk away from the river, taking the first turning on the left, **Breg**, then the third on the right, **Križevniška**, to arrive on **Trg francoske revolucije** (French Revolution Square). On the square, the **Ilirski steber** (Illyrian Column) commemorates Napoleon's Illyrian Provinces (1809–13, see *page 12*), of which Ljubljana was capital. Also here is the **Križanke poletno gledališče** (Krizanke Summer Theatre), a former monastery complex that once belonged to the Knights of the Cross. In 1956 it was converted into an open-air theatre seating 1400 (and given a retractable roof-structure in case of rain), to plans by Plečnik, and now hosts various performances from April to October, including part of the Ljubljana Festival.

Proceed north along **Vegova** to **Kongresni trg** (Congress Square), a large green square overlooked by Ljubljana University and the neighbouring **Slovenska filharmonija** (Slovenian Philharmonic Hall), built in 1891 and home to the Slovenian Philharmonic Orchestra, of which Gustav Mahler was resident conductor 1881–82. On the west side of the square, note the gilded statue of a Roman mounted on a column, a replica of the *Citizen of Emona*, the original of which is in the National Museum *(see page 28)*.

From here follow the busy thoroughfare of **Slovenska** north, then take the fourth street on the left, Štefanova, passing by the foot of the art deco **Nebotičnik** (Skyscraper) from 1933, the first high-rise building in town and the tallest in Central Europe when it was first built.

Take the second turning on the left into **Župančičeva**, then the first right, **Cankarjeva**, to arrive in front of the recently renovated **Moderna galerija**

**Above:** the Slovenian Philharmonic Hall

(Museum of Modern Art; Tues–Sat 10am–6pm, Sun 10am–1pm; admission fee; www.mg-lj.si) displaying a collection of 20th-century art including several examples of socialist realism, the preferred style in Tito's day.

Alternatively, follow Župančičeva one more street down to **Trg narodnih herojev**, home to the **Narodni muzej** (National Museum; Tues–Sun 10am–6pm, Thur until 8pm; admission fee; www.narmuz-lj.si) containing the remarkable Vače situla, a 5th-century BC bronze urn decorated with figures of men hunting, fighting and driving chariots.

## Tivoli Park

Close by, on the opposite side of the busy **Tivolska cesta**, is the entrance to the landscaped grounds of **Tivoli Park** – the safest way to reach it is to take the underpass at the end of Cankarjeva. Here, take a look in the **Muzej novejše zgodovine** (Museum of Modern History; Tues–Sun 10am–6pm; admission fee; www.muzej-nz.si), tracing Slovenian political history from the Habsburg era up to the country's declaration of independence in 1991.

In the evening, between early July and mid-August, try to attend one of the open-air performances of the Ljubljana Festival (see *Nightlife, page 80*). Dine at either **AS** *(see Eating Out, page 73)*, considered by many to be the capital's top restaurant, close to Prešeren Square, or **Spajza**, on the route up to the castle. Close the day with a late-night drink at a riverside café in the old town – **Maček** *(see Nightlife, page 77)* is the place where trendy local people go to see and be seen.

**Above Left:** the grand stairway inside the National Museum
**Above:** a family day out in Tivoli Park

## 2. KRKA VALLEY MONASTERIES *(see map, page 30)*

**A day following the course of the River Krka, east of Ljubljana. Visit the monasteries of Stična and Pleterje. Stop at an agrotourism centre for lunch, or have a picnic in the woods. There is an optional overnight stay at a castle hotel.**

*Both monasteries can be reached by public transport from Ljubljana, but if you want to see both in one day you will need a car. You should telephone in advance for a tour of Stična Monastery, and also if you wish to have lunch at the Šeruga agrotourism centre. Alternatively, pack a picnic to eat in the woods surrounding Pleterje Monastery. Take the E70 motorway east out of Ljubljana to Ivančna Gorica, 33km (21 miles) from the capital. From here, a narrow country lane leads up to the Stična Monastery, 2km (1 mile).*

Set amid gently undulating hills and green fields, is **Samostan Stična** (Sticna Monastery; daily 8am–noon, 2–5pm, museum: 8am–5pm; guided tours: Tues–Sat 8.30am, 10am, 2pm and 4pm, Sun 2pm and 4pm, advance booking essential for groups; tel: 01-787-7863; admission fee). It was founded by the Cistercians in 1135, making it the oldest monastery in Slovenia. As is customary among Cistercians, the monks lead a simple life, working the land and following a vow of silence, communicating only through sign language.

During the 15th century, the monastery was fortified against the Ottoman Turks, with 8-m (26-ft) high walls and a series of towers, and in this state of splendid isolation established itself as the most important religious, economic, educational and cultural centre in the region. In 1784 it was closed, following an edict issued by Emperor Joseph II, who ordered the dissolution of all religious orders in the region, as he believed they had become too corrupt and too powerful for the Habsburgs to control. Stična was abandoned, but the Cistercians returned in 1898. Today the monastery is in fine condition, having undergone steady reconstruction work since World War II, and is now home to around a dozen monks.

**Above:** Nova Mesto on the banks of the River Krka

## The Monastery Tour

The monastery tours begin with an informative 20-minute audio-visual presentation (in various languages, including English), after which you visit the **Slovenian Religious Museum**. It is housed in the Old Prelature, which was once the monastery's administrative centre, and is packed with an eclectic collection of religious paintings, icons, manuscripts, furniture, clocks and farm tools. From here, you are taken across the main courtyard to visit the **monastery church**. This was originally constructed in Romanesque style in the 12th century, but following a succession of later building projects it is now largely baroque. Finally, you pass through the 13th-century Gothic **vaulted cloisters** decorated with fading frescoes and encircling a garden.

At the end of the tour, visit the monastery shop, where you can buy Father Simon Ašič's herbal teas – each one said to cure a specific malady, ranging from insomnia and poor memory to cellulite – as well as the wine and honey made by the monks, and an array of religious souvenirs.

## Along the Krka Valley

Once you have seen Stična, return to Ivančna Gorica and then head for Novo mesto, taking the un-numbered secondary road rather than the E70 motorway. This scenic route follows the course of the River Krka, passing through the villages of Zagradec, Dvor and Soteska, and eventually arriving at Novo mesto.

By-pass Novo mesto, continuing along the secondary road in the direction of **Šenternej**, and on the left you will see the entrance to **Hotel Grad Otočec** (see Eating Out and Accommodation), a refurbished castle on an island accessed by a wooden bridge, where you could stop for coffee, have lunch or even stay the night (advance booking is advisable but not always essential). Or, for a taste of rural farm life, continue a short distance further, then take the turning on the right for **Ratež** to arrive at **Šeruga**

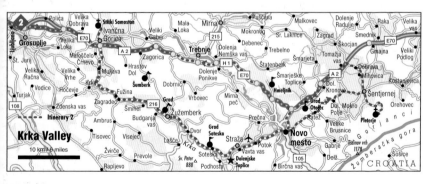

**Above:** the cloisters of Stična Monastery

*(see Eating Out and Accommodation)*, an agrotourism centre serving home-grown organic produce and also offering overnight accommodation. If you have brought a picnic, continue until you reach the woods at **Pleterje** where you will find plenty of pleasant spots to eat your lunch.

## Pleterje Monastery

Proceed to Šenternej and turn right along a winding country road to **Samostan Pleterje** (Pleterje Monastery; admission fee; www.kartuzija-pleterje.si). The church, and a multimedia exhibition, are open to visitors (daily 8am–5pm). Set in a beautiful, peaceful valley and surrounded by woods and vineyards, Pleterje was founded in 1404 by Count Herman of Celje. It belongs to Carthusian monks, an order founded by St Bruno of Cologne in the 11th century and inspired by the lifestyle of an Egyptian order of hermits. Its values include collective labour and private contemplation, vegetarianism and a vow of silence that can only be broken during a customary weekly nature walk, when the monks are allowed to converse.

During the 16th century, Pleterje was fortified against the Turks, but was abandoned in 1595, only to reopen in 1904. Because the Carthusians aim to find God in silence and solitude, much of the complex is closed to visitors, but you can view the magnificent 15th-century Gothic **Cerkev svete Trojice** (Church of the Holy Trinity), and enter the sacristy to watch a fascinating audio-visual presentation about the lifestyle of the dozen or so monks who still reside here. Be sure to call at the monastery shop (Mon–Sat), where you can buy goods produced by the monks: especially wine and several types of fiery local spirits, *žganje*, including *viljamovka,* which has a whole pear inside the bottle and *slivovka* made from plums. They also sell honey and beeswax candles (the monks keep bees).

## Open-Air Museum

End your visit by walking the same 4-km (2.5-mile) **path** around the perimeter of the complex that forms the monks' weekly walk. The route is marked with a blue circle and yellow cross, so you can follow the trail independently. While walking, close to the entrance to the monastery grounds, you will pass the **Pleterje Open-Air Museum** (Muzej na prostem Pleterje; Apr–Oct Wed–Sun, Nov–Mar Tues–Sat 10am–4pm; admission fee; www.skansen.si). Well worth a look, this cluster of traditional timber-and-thatch farm buildings has been reconstructed to create the atmosphere of 19th-century rural life.

For a rapid journey back to Ljubljana, pick up the E70 just to the north of Šenternej and head west.

**Right:** the picturesque Hotel Grad Otočec sits on its own island

# The Northwest

## 3. LAKE BLED *(see map, page 34)*

**A day in Slovenia's top resort, exploring the idyllic Lake Bled, with its picturesque island and clifftop castle, set against a backdrop of the rugged Julian Alps. There is also an optional afternoon hike to the dramatic Vintgar Gorge.**

*Try to make an early start, as this will be a busy day if you hope to cover the whole itinerary. Set off with comfortable walking shoes, swimwear, sunscreen and a towel.*

A history of tourism going back 150 years has produced a good range of accommodation options around Lake Bled, making it an ideal base for exploring the northwest. This is the first of three tours aimed at introducing visitors to the stunning mountains, valleys, lakes and rivers of Triglav National Park, which offer an exciting range of outdoor activities, such as hiking and cycling, kayaking and white-water rafting, and skiing in winter. The resort town of Bled is sedate and pristine; Lake Bohinj shows the Slovenian Alpine landscape at its most idyllic and unspoilt; and the Soča Valley follows the course of the lovely River Soča through dense pine forests and rocky gorges. Regular bus services link Ljubljana to Bled, and Bled to Bohinj; Kobarid, in the Soča Valley, is slightly more difficult to reach by public transport. Throughout summer there are bus connections, involving a change at Bovec, but if you are visiting in off-season you will need to ask for details at Bled Tourist Information Centre.

Located about 50km (30 miles) northwest of Ljubljana, Bled may be a bit too quaint and over commercialised, but the setting is truly fantastic, beside an emerald-green lake that has a little island with a church, among dense woods and with a clifftop castle, all lying snugly within a basin surrounded by spectacular mountains.

Tourism started here in 1855 when a Swiss doctor called Arnold Rikli opened thermal baths at what is now the **Grand Hotel Toplice** (see *Accommodation, page 93*). With its soothing waters, stunning natural beauty and pristine Alpine air, Bled soon became a prestigious health resort, patronised by aristocrats from all over Europe, and in the early 20th century the Yugoslav royal family built **Vila Bled** (see *Accommodation, page 93*) as their summer residence. After World War II the villa passed into the hands of Marshal Tito (who was president from 1953–80), and since 1984 it has functioned as a luxury hotel.

**Above:** sign at the entrance to the stately Vila Bled

## Bled Castle and its Museum

Begin the day with a look at the imposing **Blejski grad** (Bled Castle; daily May–Sept 8am–8pm, Oct–Apr 8am–5pm; admission fee), perched on a cliff some 100m (328ft) above the lake. Walk uphill through the centre of Bled, passing on the way **Gostilna Pri Planincu** (see *Eating Out, page 74*), where you might like to return for dinner, and **Bledec Youth Hostel** (see *Accommodation, page 92*), immediately after which you should take the signed footpath on the left. Follow a steep, winding path through the woods up to the car park and you will see the castle entrance straight ahead.

Built on a series of levels within ramparts, the castle dates back to the 11th century, although what you see now is mainly from the 16th century. Its most impressive feature is the spectacular panorama over the lake and the surrounding mountains, but the **Castle Museum** is well worth a visit for its interesting collection of period furniture, tapestries, armoury and archaeological finds. You can stop for coffee or a snack at the castle restaurant, and check out the Herbal Gallery, offering natural health products made, of course, from herbs.

## Aquatic Activities

Return to the car park and take the footpath on the right, which winds a steep, serpentine route down through the woods to the lakeside **Grajsko kopališče** (Castle Swimming Grounds; mid-June–late Sept daily 8am–7pm; admission fee). You could stop for a swim here, although the itinerary shortly reaches a more informal, and more pleasing, bathing area. Turn right to begin a 6-km (4-mile) walk anti-clockwise around the perimeter of the lake, following a waterside path lined with linden trees, horse chestnuts and weeping willows. En route you will pass the

**Above:** Bled Island in the mist
**Right:** coffee at the Grand Hotel

**Veslaški centar** (Rowing Centre), a venue for various international rowing championships and the training ground for Luka Špik and Iztok Čop, who were Olympic gold medallists in the double scull at Sydney 2000 and silver medallists at Athens 2004. Close by, the public bathing area (free), with lawns giving onto the lake, is a good place to swim and sunbathe, while the **Zaka** café-restaurant (see *Eating Out, page 74*) is a possible lunch stop, where you can sample a range of traditional Slovenian dishes.

Continue from here along the lakeside path, which is now converted into a wooden walkway for a short stretch.

## Royal Villa and Bled Island

Soon, on the right, you will see **Vila Bled** within its 5 hectares (12 acres) of landscaped gardens, with an imposing flight of steps running down to the water. When Tito was in power, he entertained an illustrious selection of foreign leaders here – India's Indira Ghandi, Ethiopia's Haile Selassie, the USSR's Nikita Krushchev and Germany's Willy Brandt, to name but a few. If you are interested in modern art, you might ask at the reception desk for permission to see Tito's projection room on the first floor. It was decorated in 1947 with an impressive cycle of frescoes painted

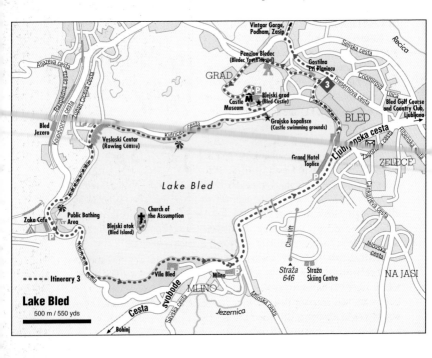

**Above:** relaxing along the lakeside path

in the bold, triumphant style of socialist realism, depicting the partisans' victory at the close of World War II, with a heroic Mother Yugoslavia waving the blue, white and red flag bearing the red star. The room is now used for meetings, and the frescoes are often covered by thick curtains.

Continue to **Mlino** (see *Eating Out, page 74*), a roadside restaurant that is popular with bikers. From the landing station outside you can either hire a rowing boat or take a guided trip on a *pletnja* (similar to a Venetian gondola) to **Blejski otok** (Bled Island) in the middle of the lake. A monumental flight of 99 steps leads from the quay up to the island's highest point, where the early Slavs built a pagan temple to Živa, their goddess of love and fertility. In the 9th century it was replaced by a pre-Romanesque Christian chapel, and in the 17th century by the baroque **Church of the Assumption** that stands here today. There's a 15th-century bell tower, and good luck is said to be in store for those who ring the bell. As you can imagine, many do so by pulling on the rope that hangs outside when they hear the legend.

## Vintgar Gorge and its Waterfalls

If you prefer hiking to boating, you could return to town and set off on a three-hour round trip to the spectacular **Vintgar Gorge** (May–Oct daily sunrise–sunset; small admission fee). To get there, take Prešerenova cesta from the centre of Bled and follow signs to **Podhom**, close to the gorge entrance. Carved by the River Radovna and flanked by rocky outcrops and birch woods, this 1.6-km (1-mile) gorge opened to the public in 1893. A series of wooden walkways and bridges follow its length, criss-crossing a succession of waterfalls and rapids along the way, culminating in the 13-m (42.5-ft) high **Šum Waterfall**. This is a popular spot, especially at weekends, and there are several snack bars and wooden tables for picnicking close by.

Return to Bled via the hilltop church of Svetega Katerina (St Catherine's) and the village of **Zasip**. The paths are easy to follow without getting lost, but if you want a detailed walking map you should call at Bled Tourist Information Centre at Cesta svobode 15b, close to Hotel Park, before setting off.

## Postcript for Golfers

A final word addressed to golfers – **Bled Golf and Country Club** (Kidričeva 10; tel: 04-537-7711; www.golf.bled.si), Slovenia's best golf course and one of the most beautiful courses in Europe, lies only 3km (2 miles) from Lake Bled. The 9-hole Lake Course involves three water hazards, and the 18-hole King's Course that was added by Donald Harradine in 1972. But be aware that if you would like to play here, you should make a reservation at least three days in advance – earlier if possible.

**Right:** rowing in the peaceful waters of Lake Bled

## 4. LAKE BOHINJ *(see map, below)*

**A day spent by Lake Bohinj, with the opportunity to take a boat trip, a cable-car ride up to the Vogel Ski Centre for spectacular views over the surrounding mountains, and an afternoon swim.**

*Bohinj is connected to Bled by a regular bus service. To explore the surroundings, you can walk, hire a bicycle, or take a boat ride across the lake. Bring good walking shoes, swimwear and a towel. Drive or take the bus from Bled to Ribčev laz on the east edge of Lake Bohinj, a distance of 26km (16 miles). En route, in the surrounding meadows, you will notice a number of the freestanding wooden hayracks that are unique to Slovenia.*

Lying inside Triglav National Park, **Bohinjsko jezero** (Lake Bohinj) is less commercialised than Bled. Building on the shores of the lake is prohibited, and in springtime the peaceful green meadows abound with wild flowers, against a backdrop of wild and rugged snow-capped Alpine peaks. It is a better base than Bled for serious hiking, thanks to its idyllic setting, the number of well-kept mountain paths, and the challenge of climbing 2,864m (9,394ft) to the apex of Slovenia's highest mountain, **Triglav**. With its three distinctive peaks (Triglav means 'three heads'), the mountain charmed the early Slavs, who believed it to be the home of a three-headed god who ruled the sky, the earth and the underworld. Today it is the symbol of Slovenia, and is featured on the national flag.

In **Ribčev laz** (No 48) you will find a Tourist Information Centre stocking a range of local walking maps, as well as various companies catering for adventure sports, and the **Hotel Jezero**. A 10-minute walk uphill from the lake stands **Hotel Bellevue**, where some of the staff still have fond memories of the time Agatha Christie stayed for several weeks in 1967 while writing *Murder on the Orient Express* (for both hotels, see *Accommodation, page 93*).

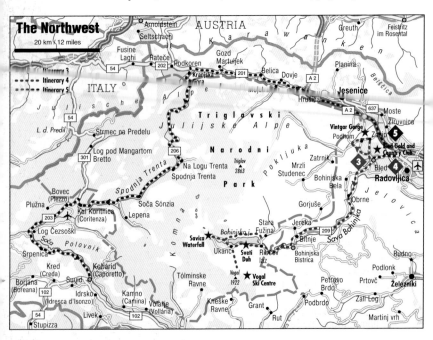

Across the road from Hotel Jezero, over a stone bridge built in 1926 (replacing an older wooden structure), check out the whitewashed medieval **Cerkev Svetega Janeza** (Church of St John the Baptist).

Churches by lakes and rivers were often dedicated to John the Baptist because of the symbolic proximity to water. The scene is at its most suggestive in the early morning, when a heavy mist often hangs over the lake. A large St Christopher is painted outside by the door. Inside are frescoes from the 15th and 16th centuries depicting the martyrdom of St John along with other scenes and characters from the Bible. However, the church is currently closed for restoration and unlikely to reopen until 2010.

## Ukanc and the Savica Waterfall

Now prepare to set off and explore the countryside surrounding the lake. From Ribčev laz, a 12-km (7-mile) walk round its perimeter takes about three hours, but there are several different ways of tackling the route and a number of optional detours on the way. At Ribčev laz 53, opposite Hotel Jezero, lies **Alpinsport** (see *Leisure Activities, page 81*) where you could hire a mountain bike as an alternative to walking. Another option, if that sounds too tiring, is to hop aboard the lake shuttle boat (May–Oct daily every 90 minutes 10am–5.30pm, journey time 30 minutes), which runs from Ribčev laz to Camp Zlatorog at **Ukanc**, 4.5km (3 miles) away on the west side of the lake.

If you decide to hike or bike, follow the main road along the south side of the lake, and after 2km (1 mile) you will pass another small whitewashed church, **Sveti Duh** (Church of the Holy Spirit). It was built in 1743 – the date

**Above:** the church of St John the Baptist beside the stone bridge. **Right:** the Savica Waterfall

is engraved above the main door – after several years of bad harvest, in the hope that it would change the tide of fortune for local farmers.

Once in Ukanc, more a cluster of holiday chalets than a village, follow the sign pointing right for Hotel Zlatorog. Just beyond the hotel lies **Erlah** (see *Eating Out, page 74*), a popular restaurant serving fresh trout at tables on an open-air terrace. Even if you don't have want to have lunch, it makes a pleasant stop for coffee. From here, a 4-km (2½-mile) marked footpath leads to **Savica Waterfall** (Slap Savica), a spectacular 97-m (318-ft) cascade cutting into a deep gorge.

## War Cemetery and the Vogel

From the main road in Ukanc, a turning on the left leads to the Vogel cable-car. A short distance along the main road is the **World War I War Cemetery** on the left, where there are over 200 graves of those – mainly Hungarians, Czechs, Slovenians, Poles and Ukrainians – who fought with the Austro-Hungarians against the Italians between 1915 and 1917.

The cable car, which is better known here as the gondola, runs daily every

30 minutes (Sept–June 8am–6pm, July–Aug 7am–6pm), ascending some 1,537m (5,000ft) to the **Vogel Ski Centre**, a stunning spot affording fantastic views over the Bohinj basin and the surrounding Alps. Just close to the point of arrival, **Planinska Koča Merjasec** (Merjasec Mountain Hut; see *Eating Out, page 74*) serves hearty local dishes, making it a perfect stop for lunch.

The winter skiing season runs from early December to late April, and Vogel offers 26km (16 miles) of ski slopes. In summer it makes a good starting point for a series of mountain walks, one of the most popular leading to the peak of **Vogel**, at a height of 1,922m (6,300ft). A walk of medium difficulty, the round trip takes about 3½ hours: If you decide to tackle it, be sure to go armed with a walking map and plenty of drinking water.

Once you have exhausted Vogel (or it has exhausted you), descend to Ukanc by cable car. From here the return journey to Ribčev laz can be achieved by boat or, if you are hiking, by completing the circuit of the lake, following the footpath along the north shore. But note that this path is closed to cyclists, so if you are biking you will have to retrace your route by road.

Back in Ribčev laz, you might like to have a swim. The best places lie on the northeast corner of the lake. Or you may choose to hire a kayak or a canoe from Alpinsport (see *Outdoor Activities, page 81*). And if Bohinj has captured your heart, which it may well have done, you could stay for dinner at **Zlatovčica** (see *Eating Out, page 74*) on the open-air terrace of Hotel Jezero, and return to Bled at nightfall.

**Above:** pastoral scene with the backdrop of the majestic Julian Alps

## 5. SOČA VALLEY *(see map, page 36)*

**A day in Kobarid. Visit the thought-provoking anti-war Kobarid Museum and take the Kobarid Historic Walk in the morning, then indulge in adventure sports on the River Soča in the afternoon.**

*This itinerary is intended as a day trip from Bled, a distance of 80km (50 miles), although you may wish to stay the preceding night in Kobarid so as to get an earlier start. In summer buses run from Bled to Bovec and Bovec to Kobarid, and there are several buses daily from Ljubljana and Nova Gorica to Kobarid, but public transport services to the river are few and far between. However, if you are booked on an X-Point activity (see page 41), they pick up in Kobarid. Be sure to contact X-Point at least a day in advance to arrange your rafting, canyoning, kayaking or canoeing trip.*

From Bled, the drive through the Alpine ski resorts of **Kranjska Gora** (39km/ 24 miles) and **Bovec** (59km/37 miles), passes through the stunning **Vršič Pass**. From Bovec onwards you are in the peaceful **Soča Valley**, following the course of the emerald-green **River Soča**, which runs from Triglav National Park to the border town of Nova Gorica (see *Itinerary 7*). This remote valley is remarkable for its excellent river-based sports – kayaking, canoeing, rafting, canyoning and fishing. You then continue to the Alpine town of Kobarid, which is set in a valley amid lush green meadows and pine forests, in the shadow of 2,244-m (7,362-ft) Mt Krn.

### The Kobarid Museum

Begin your visit to **Kobarid** with coffee on **Trg svobode**, the main square, noting **Hotel Hvala** (see *Accommodation, page 93*) where you might like to stay the night and dine on a feast of fresh fish at the highly-acclaimed **Topli Val** hotel restaurant (see *Eating Out, page 74*). Kobarid is known for two things – its museum and its adventure sports facilities – and we shall be starting with the former.

**Above:** the River Soča near Kobarid

The **Kobariški muzej** (Kobarid Museum; daily, Apr–Sept 9am–6pm, Oct–Mar 10am–5pm; admission fee; www.kobariski-muzej.si), in the 18th-century Mašer House at Gregorčičeva 10, opened in 1990 and won the European Museum of the Year award in 1993. The exhibition begins with a brief history of the region, including a hoard of miniature metal figures of Apollo and Hercules found during the excavation of an ancient Roman settlement. It also relates the amusing account of an Italian priest who visited the area in the 14th century and was shocked to find local people practising Slavic pagan rituals involving the worship of a tree and a spring of water below it – to put an end to the affair, the Catholic Church ordered that the tree in question be chopped down.

The museum then depicts the horrific events that took place in the region during World War I. When Italy entered the war in 1915, intending to advance east into Austro-Hungarian territory, the River Soča (*Izonso* in Italian) became a natural front line. Fighting in the area lasted 29 months, involved 17 nations and resulted in the deaths of an estimated 1 million soldiers and civilians.

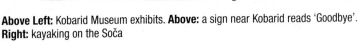

Ernest Hemingway, who was working as a volunteer ambulance driver for the Italian forces, used the experience as the basis for his novel *A Farewell to Arms*. Through photographs, maps, scale models, flags, military uniforms and weapons, the museum offers a sensitive but disturbing presentation of the fighting and its after-effects. Many visitors find they are most impressed by the 20-minute audio-visual presentation, complete with the rumble of cannons and gunfire and the flashing lights of explosions against a mountain backdrop.

**Above Left:** Kobarid Museum exhibits. **Above:** a sign near Kobarid reads 'Goodbye'.
**Right:** kayaking on the Soča

## Kobarid Historic Walk

Before leaving the museum, pick up a self-guiding pamphlet and map of the **Kobariška zgodovinska pot** (Kobarid Historic Walk; free). This well-marked 5-km (3-mile) path leads through lovely countryside, passing various World War I sites on the way. Allow about three hours to complete the circuit.

The route takes you back to the main square, then uphill to the **Italian War Memorial**, a monumental octagonal mausoleum holding the bodies of more than 7,000 Italian soldiers who were killed during World War I. It then follows the **Italian front line** where you can still distinguish trenches they dug, and passes over a hair-raising wooden suspension bridge spanning a stone canyon known as the **Soča Gorge**, leading to the impressive **Kozjak Waterfall**. Finally it brings you back to town via the so-called **Napoleon Bridge**, named to record the time when Napoleon's soldiers marched this way in the early 19th century, although the stone structure you see today was built after World War I, the older bridge having been blown up by the Austrians in 1915.

## Action Sports on the River Soča

Devote the afternoon to exploring the River Soča, with its white gravel riverbed and crystal clear, emerald-green water, which runs down from the surrounding mountains. **X-Point** (Stresova 1; tel: 05-388-5308; www.xpoint.si) organise rafting, canyoning, kayaking and canoeing trips. The season runs from May to September, and all trips operate subject to weather conditions. For rafting and canyoning you must know how to swim, and there must be a minimum of three people, although individuals can often join up with an existing group. Rafting trips last a total of 2½ hours and all the necessary equipment is provided – just bring swimwear and a T-shirt. Canyoning trips last approximately 3 hours, and, once again, all equipment is provided, although you should bring your own sports shoes if possible. Groups meet in the centre of Kobarid (usually at 10am or 2pm) then drive to the river by minibus. X-Point can also arrange paragliding, mountain biking and hiking tours, including a two-day hike from Bohinj to Kobarid, which you could use to combine Itineraries 4 and 5.

# The Southwest

## 6. PIRAN, PORTOROŽ AND THE SEČOVLJE SALTPANS *(see map, pages 44–45)*

**A day exploring the Slovenian coast, from the lovingly preserved Venetian-Gothic town of Piran to the commercial seaside resort of Portorož, concluding with a tour of the Sečovlje Saltworks Museum.**

*If you are based in Piran, this trip can be done on foot, although hiring a bicycle will make the visit to the saltworks far more enjoyable. You will need your passport to visit the Saltworks Museum, which lies beyond the Slovenian border checkpoint.*

There is no better way to begin a day on the Slovenian coast than with morning coffee in **Piran**, seated outside the **Café Teater** at Stjenkova 1, overlooking the harbour. With its Venetian-Gothic houses perched on a small peninsula, capped with a lighthouse and presided over by a hilltop church, Piran is the undisputed pearl of the Slovenian coast, which stretches 47km (29 miles) between the borders with Italy and Croatia. The town remains culturally and spiritually connected to Italy, thanks to almost 500 years of Venetian rule. The name Piran dates back much further, to the days when the ancient Greeks lit fires on the tip of the peninsula (*pyr* being Greek for fire) to guide ships to the port at Aegida (present-day Koper).

## Tartini Square and St George's Church

Just a few steps back from the harbour, the Old Town centres on the beautiful **Tartinijev trg** (Tartini Square), which formed an inner harbour until it was land-filled in 1864. The white marble paving was laid down in 1990. The piazza is named after the violinist and composer Giuseppe Tartini (1692–1770), who was born in the yellow building (No 7) now housing a **Tartini Memorial Room** (July–Aug Tues–Sun 9am–noon, 6–9pm, Sept–June 11am–noon, 5–6pm; www.pmk-kp.si). The composer lived most of his adult life in Italy, where he wrote more than 300 pieces for violin. In the centre of the piazza, which has excellent acoustics and hosts open-air performances in summer, stands a larger-than-life bronze statue of Tartini, erected in 1896.

    Overlooking the square are the superbly located **Hotel Tartini** (see *Accommodation, page 93*), a rather pompous-looking neo-Renaissance

**Above:** Piran's Venetian-style harbour

# piran, portorož and the saltpans

**Town Hall** built in 1877 by the Habsburgs; and, at No 2, a useful **Tourist Information Centre**.

However, the oldest and best-loved building here is undoubtedly the red, three-storey **Benečanka hiša** (Venetian House) at No 4, with ornate Venetian-Gothic windows. Legend has it that in the 15th century a rich Venetian merchant fell in love with a beautiful local girl and, despite the jealousy and gossip of some of the townspeople, built her this house, with its strategically-placed corner balcony, so he could see her when he sailed into the harbour. Between the two windows on the top floor an inlaid stone is engraved with a lion (the symbol of Venice) and the words '*lassa pur dir*' ('let them talk').

Leave the square by **IX Korpusa**, running behind the Benečanka, walk uphill and turn left onto **Adamičeva**, to arrive at the 17th-century baroque **Cerkev svetli Jurji** (Church of St George). It is currently under renovation, and will be for several years to come, but look in the adjoining **Parish Museum** to see several reliquaries, supposedly containing body parts of its namesake, St George, the city's patron: a silver-clad right leg and a silver box containing two of the saint's teeth. Also note a splendid silver statue of the saint astride a rearing horse, slaying the mythical dragon.

Next to the church, the freestanding **bell tower** (summer daily 10am–noon, 4–8pm; admission fee) also has Venetian influences, being a scaled-down copy of the campanile of San Marco in Venice. Climb to the top for panoramic views, with Italy to the northwest and Croatia to the south. An octagonal **Baptistery** from 1650 completes the church complex.

## Historic Seafront and the Maritime Museum

From here, **Adamičeva** follows the ridge along the peninsula to bring you back down to the town. If you turn right at the bottom you will arrive on **Prešernova nabrežje**, the seafront promenade, which is lined with characteristic pastel-coloured façades. Stroll the perimeter of the peninsula in an anti-clock-wise direction, noting the **baroque tower**, once a lighthouse, at its tip, the Punta.

Turn left, back into the warren of narrow cobbled streets, to reach **Gregorčičeva**, then turn right for **Trg 1 Maja**, which was Piran's main square in medieval times. Today it is rimmed by baroque façades, overlooking a central cistern with two wells, built in 1775, where gutters from the surrounding rooftops channelled water to be stored in case of drought. Also here, you will find **Cantina** (see *Eating Out, page 74*).

**Above:** a restaurant by the sea
**Right:** Tartini's statue in the square named after him

the southwest

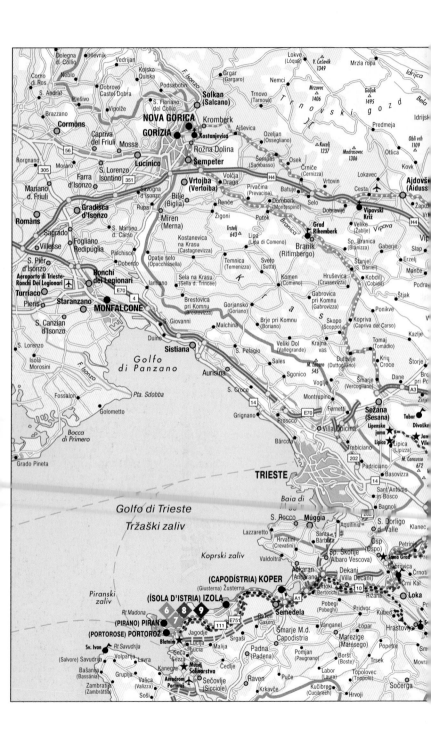

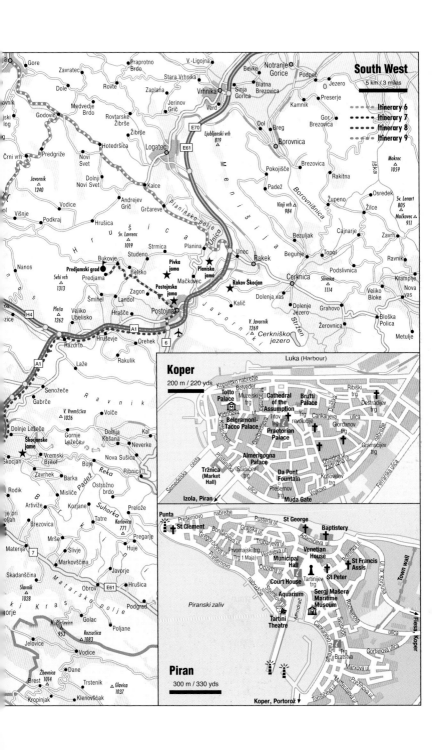

**South West**

5 km / 3 miles

············ Itinerary 6
–––––––––– Itinerary 7
–––––––––– Itinerary 8
·–·–·–·–·– Itinerary 9

**Koper**

200 m / 220 yds

Luka (Harbour)

Kopališko nabrežje

Totto Palace
Belveder
Muzejski trg
Cathedral of the Assumption
Brutti Palace
Ribiški trg
Destradijev trg
Belgramoni-Tacco Palace
Titov trg
Trg revolucije
Cankarjeva trg
Giordanov trg
Praetorian Palace
Almerigogna Palace
Obzidna ul.
Zadružna ul.
Gramscijev trg
Tržnica (Market Hall)
Stanicev trg
Da Pont Fountain
Kosovelov trg
Ferrarska ulica
Prešernov trg
Vokovo
Muda Gate

Izola, Piran

**Piran**

300 m / 330 yds

Punta
Prešernovo nabrežje
Pusteria ul.
St George
Baptistery
St Clement
Bonifacijeva ul.
Gljalska ul.
Gregorčičeva ul.
Trubarjeva ul.
Verdieva ul.
Adamičeva ul.
Venetian House
St Francis Assis
Prvomajski trg (Trg 1 Maja)
Municipal Hall
Obzidna ul.
St Peter
Court House
Tartinijev trg
Seraj Mašera Maritime Museum
Aquarium
Piranski zaliv
Tartini Theatre
Trg Bratstva
Marxova ul.
Koper, Portorož
Town wall
Fiesa, Koper

Leave the square via **Verdijeva**, passing yet another notable restaurant, **Verdi** (see *Eating Out, page 75*) and return to Tartinjev trg. Walk towards the harbour then turn left to follow the seafront promenade away from the town

centre. Immediately on your left, at Cankarjevo nabrežje 3, is the **Pomorski muzej Sergej Mašera** (Sergej Mašera Maritime Museum; summer Tues–Sun 9am–noon, 6–9pm, winter Tues–Sun 9am–noon, 3–6pm; admission fee). Well worth a visit, this enlightening museum traces Piran's historic connections with the sea through a collection of model ships, sailor's uniforms and navigational equipment.

If you're ready for a lunchtime snack, call at **Barka** (see *Eating Out, page 74*), just off Tartinijev trg, for Balkan-style fast food.

## To Portoroz

Set off along the coastal promenade, overlooked by a number of large modern hotels, to **Portorož**, 3km (2 miles) away. It is a pleasant walk, but for the afternoon visit to the saltworks you might consider hiring a bike, either from News Café Bernadin at Obala 41 (tel: 05-674-1004), or Atlas Express at Obala 55 (tel: 05-674-6772), both of which you will pass en route.

A concrete-and-neon resort popular with middle-aged Europeans and nouveaux-riche Russians, Portorož first attracted foreign visitors in the late 19th century when ailing Austro-Hungarians came to wallow in the mud baths and saltwater pools. In 1912 the **Hotel Palace** opened but by the turn of the century was in a state of dereliction, having been abandoned for over a decade. It was bought by the Slovenian petrol company Istrabenz and

has been restored to something approaching its former glory. The largest and most expensive establishment here is the **Grand Hotel Palace** (see *Accommodation, page 93*), the modern neighbour of the original, which offers plush rooms and a luxurious Wellness Centre. In fact, Portorož now specialises in beauty treatments, and there are a number of private clinics offering cosmetic surgery at prices lower than those in Western Europe or the United States.

Proceed along the main road through Lucija, and look out for a narrow road on the left leading uphill to the settlement of Korte. If you have still not had lunch, hike or bike up to this village noted for its vineyards, and call at **Gostilna Korte** (see *Eating Out, page 75*).

## The Saltworks Museum

Spend the afternoon at the **Muzej solinarstva** (Saltworks Museum; Apr–Oct 9am–6pm; admission fee; www.kpss.si) on the Sečovlje Salt Pans. To reach it, follow the main road south, cross the Slovenian border checkpoint (be sure to have your passport at hand), then turn right just before the Croatian checkpoint, to follow an unsurfaced track for 3km (2 miles) across an eerie, flat, wet landscape criss-crossed by channels and dykes and visited by a number of rare bird species.

The salt pans were founded in the 13th century and covered 650 hectares (1,600 acres) until they were abandoned in 1967. They were dotted with some 400 stone cottages, where salt workers lived from late April to late September. Two of these dwellings have been restored to form exhibition spaces.

'Piran was built on salt', local people say. The business took off in the mid-14th century, when a new production method was introduced by salt workers from the island of Pag (in present-day Croatia). By employing a mixture of micro-organisms and gypsum (called *petola*), which forms a layer between the mud and the crystalised salt, they were able to make the salt whiter and purer and therefore of higher market value. The parish of Piran was entitled to one-seventh of the salt produced, the salt workers to one-fifth, and the rest went to the Venetian Republic, which monopolised the salt business on the Adriatic. To protect the market, anyone found smuggling salt had their cargo and ship confiscated, and even risked years of hard labour as a galley slave.

## An Evening in Piran

Return to Piran for the early evening. If you are here between mid-August and mid-September, check out the Tartini Festival programme for cultural entertainment (www.tartinifestival.org). Dine at **Neptun** (see *Eating Out, page 75*) then enjoy a glass of wine on the floodlit Tartinjev trg at **Cantina Zizola**. If you wish to party into the small hours, Slovenia's largest open-air nightclub, **Ambasada Gavioli** (see *Nightlife, pages 79*), is only a few kilometres down the road from Piran, at Izola.

**Above Left:** taking a break in Tartinjev trg. **Left:** residential area of Portorož **Right:** all set for the evening promenade in Piran

## 7. IDRIJA AND NOVA GORICA *(see map, page 44)*

**A day driving north of the coast to visit Idrija, famed for mercury min-
ing and lace making; and Nova Gorica, a new town on the border with
Italy, known for its 24-hour casinos. There's an optional stop at the fortified hill town of Štanjel on the return journey.**

*You need a car for this trip as there are no direct bus links. Set off early
from Piran to reach Idrija in time for the 10am tour of Idrija Mercury Mine.
Take the main road from the coast heading towards Ljubl-
jana, pass the junction for Postojna and continue northeast as far as Rakek, where you should turn left for Idrija.*

Lying in a valley at the confluence of the River Idri-
jca and the River Nikova, **Idrija** is Slovenia's oldest mining town. Mercury – the only metal that exists
in a liquid state at room temperature, hence its common name, quicksilver – was discovered here in 1490.
The town, which was fortunately gifted with a plentiful supply of water and timber, essential for the
extraction of mercury, grew as the mine shafts extended
underground, attracting workers from other regions
of the Habsburg Empire. When production reached it
peak in the second half of the 18th century, Idrija was
providing 13 percent of the world's mercury.

In the past mercury was used in the production of
silver and gold, in batteries, light bulbs, tooth fillings
and medicine. Today it is regarded as a serious pol-
lutant, capable of damaging the human brain, and
its use is being gradually phased out. The last mine
closed in 1999, by which time the price had fallen so low
that production was no longer profitable.

You can take a 1 ½-hour guided tour of **Antonijev rov** (Idrija Mercury
Mine; Mon–Fri 10am and 3pm, Sat–Sun 10am, 3pm and 4pm; admission
fee; www.rzs-idrija.si). The mine, which dates back to 1500, is entered
through a house at Arkova 43, where you will be provided with an over-
coat and a helmet. The tour consists of an interesting audio-visual presentation about the history of the town and the mine, then a walk along a 1.2-km
(¾-mile) circular route descending 22m (72ft) below ground level, where
your guide will explain how the miners worked and show you an unusual
18th-century underground chapel.

### Lace-making Heritage

While the men of Idrija worked the mines, their womenfolk mastered
the skills of bobbin lace, a craft brought here by Czech and German mining families. The craft is still alive today, and there are a number of small
boutiques on Mestni trg, the main square, where you can buy lace – try
**Studio Irma Vončina** at Mestni trg 17. Each year in late June, Idrija hosts
a **Lacemaking Festival** (see *Calendar of Events, page 84*), when stalls are
set up on Mestni trg displaying lace and offering visitors the local culinary

**Above:** a figure in the Mercury Mine museum

speciality *žlikrofi* (potato balls flavoured with marjoram and wrapped in pasta, very similar to Italian ravioli).

Lace-making and the mining industry are also covered extensively in the **Mestni muzej** (Town Museum; daily 9am–6pm; admission fee; www.muzej-idrija-cerkno.si), in **Gewerkenegg Castle**, which was built in 1533 as the mine's administrative centre and still dominates the town. For a late lunch, you could call at **Restauracija Barbara** (Mon–Fri 4–10pm; see *Eating Out, page 75*) where you can sample some Idrijan specialities such as *žlikrofi* and *sukavc* (cabbage soup).

## Nova Gorica

Leave Idrija the way you came in, and after a short distance, turn right at **Godovič**, driving west through **Ajdovščina** and **Šempas** to reach **Nova Gorica**, 50km (31 miles) from Idrija. After World War II, the 1946 Paris Peace Conference ceded the region of Primorska to Yugoslavia, but the town of Gorizia remained in Italy. Tito immediately set about building a new town, employing youth brigades to construct the concrete apartment blocks and landscape the parks you see today. The two neighbouring towns grew side by side, divided by political ideals and separated by a fence, leading some observers to compare the situation to that in Berlin, but the Yugoslav regime was nowhere near as strict as that imposed on the Eastern bloc.

The only part of Gorizia that Yugoslavia kept was the railway station, which dates from 1906, making it Nova Gorica's oldest building. At midnight on 30 April 2004, on the eve of Slovenia's entrance to the EU, the European Commission President Romano Prodi and the Slovenian Prime Minister Anton Rop met at **Piazza Transalpina** in front of the station to celebrate the opening up of the border. Piazza Transalpina now has a mosaic depicting the reunification. Despite its interesting past, Nova Gorica is rather dreary, the main attraction being its numerous casinos. Casinos are largely banned in Italy, so Italians hop over the border to try their luck. Slovenia's largest casino is in the **Hotel Casino Perla** (see *Accommodation, page 94*).

## Fortified Hill Town

Alternatively, on the return journey to Piran you could stop at **Štanjel**, 28km (18 miles) southeast of Nova Gorica. This lovely fortified hill town, with a grey-stone castle and a 17th-century church, is one of the oldest settlements in the Karst region. **Grad Štanjel** (Štanjel Castle) hosts the Lojže Spacal Gallery (Galerija Lojže Spacala; summer Tues–Fri 10am–2pm, Sat–Sun 10am–6pm, winter Tues–Fri 11am–2pm, Sat–Sun 11am–5pm) displaying paintings of the local Karst landscape. Return to the coast for dinner.

**Above:** hand-made lace for sale

## 8. THE KARST *(see map, pages 44–45)*

**A day in the Karst area, beginning with the mysterious underground world of Postojna Cave, then on to Predjama to visit a castle built into a sheer cliff face. Round off the day with the magnificent white Lipizzaner horses at Lipica Stud Farm.**

*There is a regular bus service from Piran to Postojna (all Ljubljana buses pass through here), but to complete the entire itinerary you really need a car. To make the most of this day, set off from Piran by 8.30am so that you reach the cave for the 10am tour, and, if you can, try to plan your trip for a day when there's a dressage display at Lipica Stud Farm (Apr–Oct Tues, Fri and Sun 3pm). Bring a warm jacket or good pullover for the cave tour, whatever the weather outside.*

From Piran follow the main road northeast to **Postojna**, 73km (45 miles), driving through the Karst area, a landscape of vineyards, pine woods and grey limestone villages. The word *karst* originated here, and has been adopted internationally as the term for this type of limestone area, characterised by geological phenomena such as sink holes, underground streams and caves with stalactites and stalagmites.

### Postojna Cave

Lying 1.5km (1 mile) northwest of Postojna, **Postojnska jama** (Postojna Cave; daily, Nov–Mar 10am, noon, 3pm, early Apr, Oct 10am, noon, 2pm, 4pm, late Apr–Sept on the hour 10am–5pm, with 9am tours May–Sept and 6pm tours June–Aug; admission fee; www.postojna-cave.com). This cave is well-worth seeing, as it is one of the most monumental and beautiful examples of the Karst underworld. Carved out by the River Pivka some 2 million years ago, it comprises more than 20km (12 miles) of underground tunnels and grottoes – of which you will visit only a small part – complete with stalactites and stalagmites.

**Above:** visiting the spectacular Postojna Cave

Open to the public for almost 200 years, it has received some 30 million visitors. When the great British sculptor Henry Moore came here in 1955, he left a message in the visitors' book saying, 'This is the best exhibition of Nature's sculpture I have ever seen'.

An electric train takes visitors through 3.5km (2 miles) of beautifully lit sculpted galleries, chambers and halls, followed by a 1.5km (1 mile) guided tour on foot (available in English). A highlight is the giant Koncertna Dvorna (Concert Hall), a space with exceptional acoustic qualities that hosts occasional concerts for audiences of up to 10,000, and at Christmas stages a 'living crèche' accompanied by carol singing. Visits last 1½ hours, and the subterranean temperatures remain at a steady 10ºC (50ºF) all year; if you forget to bring a jacket, you can hire a felt cloak at the entrance. Photography is prohibited, but you can buy a video or DVD of the cave in the shop at the end of the tour.

Before leaving, take a look in the Speleobiological Station, lying 50m (160ft) from the cave entrance. Here you can see a multimedia presentation about the karst, and a vivarium containing live specimens of cave fauna. Look out for the *proteus anguinus*, a blind, flesh-pink salamander that can live for years without eating, and, due to its bizarre appearance, is commonly known as the 'human fish'.

## Predjama Castle

Proceed now to **Predjama**, which is located 7km (4 miles) northwest of Postojna Cave. Above the village, built into the face of a rocky cliff, nestles the stunningly photogenic **Predjamski grad** (Predjama Castle; daily, Nov–Mar 10am–4pm, Apr, Oct 10am–6pm, May–Sept 9am–6pm, July until 7pm, Aug until 9pm; admission fee; www.turizem-kras.si). There has been a castle here since the early 13th century, although the four-storey building you see today dates from the 16th century. Inside, staircases to the upper floors are carved from the solid bedrock, several rooms are arranged with period furniture, and below the castle there is a cave, which can be visited at certain hours during peak season.

In the 15th century, Predjama was home to Erasmus, a Robin Hood-type character. The governor of Triest tracked Erasmus down to Predjama and held the castle under siege, little knowing that it had a secret tunnel leading to the village of Vipava. Erasmus and his men would humiliate their adversaries by throwing fresh fruit from the castle windows. Erasmus's memory lives on in the form of the **Erasmus Knights' Tournament** (see *Calendar of Events, page 85*).

**Above:** Predjama Castle blends into the rocky cliff

Retrace your path back to Postojna. If you are hungry and don't mind the tour groups, stop at **Jamska**, near the cave entrance, for lunch. If you would prefer to lunch with local people, return to the main road for Koper, take the turning on the right for **Divača**, then follow the signs to **Lokev**, where you will find **Gombač**. (For both restaurants, see *Eating Out, page 75.*) Be sure to try some of the Teran red wine, for which the Karst area is renowned.

After lunch, carry on to **Lipica**, to visit the stud farm.

On the way you will pass signs to **Škocjanske jame** (Škocjan caves), Slovenia's second biggest cave attraction and a possible alternative to Lipica for the dedicated cave fan. Guided tours are 3km (2 miles) long and the path is rough in places (daily, June–Sept on the hour 10am–5pm, Nov–Feb 10am and 1pm plus 3pm on Sun, Apr–May, Oct 10am, 1pm, 3.30pm; admission fee; www.park-skocjanske-jame.si).

## Lipica Stud Farm

**Kobilarna Lipica** (Lipica Stud Farm; guided tours on the hour, July–Aug daily 9–11am and 1–6pm, Apr–June and Sept–Oct Mon–Fri 9–11am, 1–5pm, Sat–Sun 9–11am, 1–6pm, Nov–Feb daily 10–11am, 1–3pm, Mar Mon–Fri 10–11am, 1–3pm, Sat–Sun 10am–11am, 1–4pm, ; admission fee; www.lipica.org) is the original birthplace of the white Lipizzaner horses, which most famously perform at the Spanish Riding School of Vienna (although since 1920 their horses have been bred in Piber in Austria). The farm here was founded in 1580 by the Habsburgs, who brought Berber horses from Spain (hence the name, the 'Spanish' Riding School of Vienna), where they had originally come with the Moors from North Africa. These Berber horses were crossed with Arabians and local Karst horses – hardy stock that the Romans once used to pull chariots – to produce the Lipizzaner.

Noted for their gentle nature, beauty, agility and great willingness to learn, these horses are born black or brown, and turn white around the age of seven. They stand 15–15.3 hands high (around 1.55m/5ft at the shoulder), have long, powerful backs and strong muscular necks, and can be trained to perform intricate dressage steps such as the pirouette and piaffe.

To really appreciate the dexterity of these horses, try to catch them and their riders in action as they perform a dressage display (Apr–Oct Tues, Fri and Sun 3pm). You can also visit training sessions (Apr–Oct Tues–Sun 10am–noon). And if you want to experience riding a Lipizzaner yourself, with prior arrangement you can ride out with a guided group or have a riding lesson.

You could decide to stay here overnight – Lipica has two hotels, as well as pools, tennis courts and a golf course. Otherwise, you must make the 57-km (36-mile) return journey to Piran for the evening.

**Above:** the famous Lipizzaner horses

## 9. KOPER AND HRASTOVLJE *(see map, page 44–45)*

**This itinerary takes you to the Italianate port town of Koper, once the Venetian Empire's main centre in Istria, then inland to the village of Hrastovlje, home to a Romanesque church decorated with a cycle of stunning 15th-century frescoes.**

*If you wish to follow the entire route outlined here, this trip should be done by car, but Koper is connected to Piran by a regular bus service, so the first part of the itinerary is easily manageable for those without their own transport.*

Leave Piran in the morning, following the main road 17km (10 miles) northeast to **Koper**, the most important city on the Slovenian coast and the country's main port. Uninspiring industrial suburbs conceal an enchanting old medieval town, which was an island until 1825 when it was joined to the mainland, first by a causeway and later by a landfill project.

The earliest settlement, Aegida, founded by the ancient Greeks, was followed by the Roman Capris. The Byzantines fortified the town and called it Justinopolis. In 1279, it was taken by the Venetians, under whom it remained for over 500 years, becoming the capital of Venetian Istria, with the Italian name, Capodistria.

### Titov trg and the Cathedral

Enter the old town through the Renaissance **Porta della Muda** (Muda Gate). Built in 1516 in the style of a triumphal arch opening onto **Prešernov trg**, this has always been Koper's main entrance. At the top end of the square stands an octagonal baroque fountain dating from 1666, when Koper was an island. Maintaining a fresh

**Above:** Titov trg, Koper
**Left:** Venetian influence

water supply was a constant problem for the island's 10,000 or so inhabitants, and water had to be conducted to the fountain from a spring on the mainland, via pipes under the sea.

Turn left at the top of the square onto **Županičeva**, noting **Istrska klet** (see *Eating Out, page 76*), where you might return for an informal lunch, then right onto **Čeviljarska** to enter the main square, **Titov trg**, through an arch-

way formed by the Praetorian Palace. Koper's most outstanding monuments are grouped around this beautiful piazza. Take a break to enjoy the spectacle over coffee at the **Loggia Café**, which has occupied the ground floor of the arcaded Venetian-Gothic **Loggia** since 1864. Originally erected in 1462, the loggia's present appearance dates from the late 17th century. On the opposite side of the square, the **Praetorian Palace** is a mix of Venetian-Gothic and Renaissance styles. It was once the home of Koper's *podesta* (mayor), who was appointed annually by the Doge of Venice from among Venetian nobles, and also functioned as the seat of the Grand Council, which was made up of local aristocracy. Restored in 2001, it now houses the **Tourist Information Centre** on the ground floor (No 3).

The east side of the square is dominated by the **Cathedral of the Assumption** (Stolnica Marijinega vnebovzetja; daily 7am–noon, 4–7pm; free) founded in 1186 when Koper became an independent diocese, although what you see today dates from a succession of later building projects. The façade bears three Venetian-Gothic arches at ground level, which are now filled in, but would once have formed an open porch, while the upper level is Renaissance. Inside, note several paintings by the renowned Venetian artist Vittore Carpaccio (1465–1526), who lived in Koper in his later years. The 36-m (118-ft) **bell tower** (daily 10am–1pm, 4–7pm; admission fee) dates from 1664 – climb to the top for stunning views. Behind the cathedral lies the 12th-century circular **Baptistery**.

## The Koper Museum and Carpacciov trg

Leave Titov trg via **Kidričeva**, stopping at No 19 to look in the **Pokrajinski Muzej Koper** (Koper Regional Museum; July–Aug Tues–Sun 9am–1pm, 6–9pm, Sept–June Tues–Fri 10am–6pm, Sat–Sun 9am–1pm; admission fee; www.pmk-kp.si), for a display of stone carvings from local churches, portraits, period furniture, a painting of how Koper looked when it was still an island, and the highlight, a copy of the *Danse Macabre* from the Church of the Holy Trinity in Hrastovlje (*see page 55*).

Proceed along Kidričeva to arrive on **Carpacciov trg**, named after the Venetian artist, and you'll find **Carpaccio House** (No 6) where he is said to have lived. In the middle of the square, **St Justina's Column** records the fact that Koper was one of several Venetian-ruled port towns to send a

**Above:** frescoes in the Church of the Holy Trinity in Hrastovlje
**Right:** the Romanesque church and defensive walls, Hrastovlje

galleon to the 1571 Battle of Lepanto, at which the Turkish navy met massive defeat. On the west side of the square, a 15th-century salt warehouse separates the old town from the seafront.

## Hrastovlje

Devote the afternoon to **Hrastovlje**, an inland village lying 22km (14 miles) east of Koper. To reach it, take the road northeast of Koper in the direction of Spodnje Škofije, turning right at the main junction for Dekani and Rižana. Once you have passed through Rižana, turn right again for Hrastovlje, driving through typical Istrian countryside until you reach this cluster of terracotta-roofed cottages.

On a small hill above the village stands **Cerkev svete Trojice** (Church of the Holy Trinity), a Romanesque church hidden behind 16th-century defensive walls, intended to protect it against the Ottoman Turks, and to offer a place of refuge in the event of an attack. The church is usually open throughout the day, but if you should find it locked, call at house No 30 and ask for the key. Inside, the walls are entirely covered with frescoes in rich, warm, muted blues, greens, reds and yellows. They were painted in 1490 by Janez iz Kastva, although they were only rediscovered – beneath several layers of whitewash – during the 1950s. The best known piece is the grotesque *Danse Macabre* (Dance of Death), showing how we are all equal in the face of the Grim Reaper, while other pieces include *The Creation*, the *Journey of the Magi*, the *Last Judgement*, other Biblical scenes and images of saints. There is also the *Calendar Cycle* on the ceiling depicting the agricultural and domestic activities appropriate to each month of the year, providing a glimpse into the lives of those who once lived in this rural area. Note the medieval graffiti scratched on the walls – the unusual script is Glagolitic, the predecessor to Cyrillic, which was used in the early Slavonic church.

Your sightseeing over for the day, return to Piran for dinner.

# *The East*

## 10. MARIBOR *(see map, page 57)*

**This is an excursion to discover Maribor, Slovenia's second city (after Ljubljana). The morning is spent in the old town, and the afternoon is given over to bathing at Maribor Island on the River Drava.**

*If you wish to see the Vinag wine cellars, be sure to book a visit in advance. The best way to reach the island is to hire a bicycle. You will probably want to swim, so bring a towel, swimwear and a picnic. There is a frequent fast train service linking Ljubljana and Maribor.*

The city of Maribor, although generally more geared towards business travellers than tourists, is the obvious launching pad for the three itineraries covering the east of Slovenia. In contrast to the mountainous northwest and the karst and coast of the southwest, this part of the country is typically Central European, and the influences of Vienna and Budapest are apparent everywhere, in the architecture, the food and the wine. Between Maribor and Ptuj lies the flat, fertile flood plain of the River Drava. Northeast of Ptuj the landscape softens into undulating green hills, and it is here, along the Jeruzalem wine road, that Slovenia's best white wines are produced. South of Maribor, close to the border with Croatia, the country's oldest spa town, Rogaška Slatina, offers a variety of health and beauty treatments as well as recreation and relaxation.

Maribor lies on the left bank of the River Drava, 128km (79 miles) northeast of Ljubljana. With its coloured baroque façades and steep-pitched terracotta roofs it has a distinctly bourgeois feel, and local people are quick to point out that after World War II, while Ljubljana attracted migrant workers from the other republics of Yugoslavia, Maribor remained a stronghold of wealthy old Slovenian families who had prospered under the Habsburgs. In fact, here you will find that the older generation are likely to speak German, but not English.

### Town Square and the City Castle

Begin the day with morning coffee at the green-fronted **Astoria kavarna** at Slovenska 2, for decades a favourite local meeting place, on the edge of **Grajska trg** (Castle Square), which functioned as the main square in medieval

times. If you have a sweet tooth, proceed a couple of doors down from Astoria to Slovenska 6, where **Kavarna Ilich**, a *slaščičarna* (cake shop), has been in business since 1909, producing delicious pastries.

Grajska trg runs into **Trg svobode** (Freedom Square), overlooked by **Mestni grad** (City Castle) built

**Left:** Maribor's imposing Town Hall
**Above right:** a café in Glavni trg

by Emperor Frederik III in the late 15th century. In medieval times a castle, no longer in existence, was built on Piramida, the hill to the north of the present centre. Maribor grew up below it, and was fortified in the 14th century against the Hungarians and the Turks. The City Castle was incorporated into the existing fortification system and, although the old town walls were demolished in the late 19th century, three of the towers remain.

The castle now houses the **Pokrajinski muzej Maribor** (Maribor Regional Museum; Tues–Sat 9am–4pm, Sun 9am–2pm; admission fee; www.pmuzej-mb.si), and the baroque rooms, decorated with stucco work and frescoes, are filled with a large collection of regional costumes, objects representing Maribor's various guilds, wine-making tools, archaeological finds, paintings and sculpture. In the main room, the Knights' Hall, the Hungarian composer and pianist Franz Liszt (1811–86) gave a concert in 1847.

## Wine Tastings

Close to the castle, at Trg svobode 3, lie the **Vinagova vinska klet** (Vinag Wine Cellars; tel: 02-220-8111; admission fee; www.vinag.si). For a tour and a wine tasting session you need to book in advance, and the easiest way to do so is through the Tourist Information Centre. The cellars, built

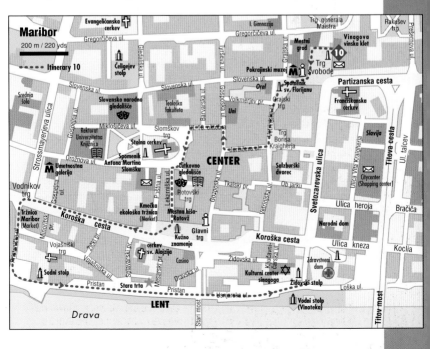

in the mid-19th century, are among the largest in Central Europe. They have a storage capacity for 5.5 million litres (1.5 million gallons), lie 7m (23ft) below ground, and comprise 2.5km (1.5 miles) of dark tunnels, lined with old oak barrels and huge modern metal containers. The walls are covered with a black mould – which is good, even if it doesn't look it: it indicates that the temperature (12°C/54°F) and humidity are correct. Most of the wines here are white – laški rizling, chardonnay, sauvignon, pinot blanc, traminer and pinot noir – and the local favourite, Mariborčan, is made from blending all six. The cellars also produce Plenina Royal, which is a sparkling wine made by the classical champagne process of turning the bottles, freezing them, cutting them open, then rebottling the wine. The *arhivo* (vintage wine store) contains bottles dating back as far as 1946 –

during World War II the Germans stole or drank what was already there, so no earlier vintages remain.

Return to Grajksi trg, leaving from the street at the bottom end, **Vetrinjksi**. Take the first on the right, **Jurčičeva**, then the first on the right again, to arrive on **Gosposka**, Maribor's main shopping street. As you walk up Gosposka, the vineyards north of town on Piramida are clearly visible. Local people say that the wine flows straight down from Piramida and into their glasses – which sounds like a good idea.

### The Cathedral and Main Square

Take the first on the left, **X Oktobra**, to arrive on **Slomškov trg** (Slomšek Square), a green square focusing on a central garden with plenty of trees and the cream-coloured, Gothic **Stolna cerkev** (Cathedral). In medieval times the cobbled area in front of the cathedral was a graveyard, but the only trace that remains of it today is a stone 'Pillar of Eternal Light'. Inside the cathedral you can see the tomb of Anton Martin Slomšek, Bishop of Maribor in the late 19th century. In 1999 Slomšek was beatified, and the stained-glass windows commemorate his life, as well as the visit to the city that year of Pope John Paul II.

As you step out of the cathedral turn left and take **Lekarniška** to arrive on **Glavni trg** (Main Square). In the centre stands the ornate, baroque **Kužno znamenje** (Plague Pillar) featuring six saints, each said to protect against illness, grouped around a central column capped by a golden figure of the Virgin Mary. It was designed by Jožef Straub in 1743, at a time when the plague had just claimed one-third of the population. Also on the square, note the 16th-century **Rotovž** (Town Hall) which now hosts **Toti rotovž** (see *Eating Out, page 76)*, where you might return for dinner.

Walk the length of the square, away from the centre, and follow **Koroška** then turn left to arrive on **Vodnikov trg**, home to the **open-air market**

**Above:** the Plague Pillar in Glavni trg. **Above right:** flags outside the Town Hall.
**Right:** a view of the town from across the River Drava

(Mon–Sat 7am–2pm), where the stalls – many of them run by gypsies – display a colourful array of seasonal fruit and vegetables, and a selection of hand-crafted wooden products, as well as clothes and household items.

## Along the River Drava

Follow **Pristaniška** down to the **River Drava**, and on the left you will see the white cylindrical **Sodni stolp** (Judicial Tower), where trials were once held. From here continue along the waterside promenade, known as **Lent**, towards the bridges. This was once the loading station for wine and timber, which from the 13th century onwards were transported by raft down the Drava to Osijek and Belgrade. Later, Maribor prospered still further, as all vessels sailing from Austria towards the Black Sea were obliged to stop here for one night and pay port tax – taverns and brothels opened to cater to the seamen, and flourished. However, water transport declined with the advent of the railways in the late 19th century, and ceased altogether after World War II when sections of the Drava were dammed to control the flow of water driving the new hydroelectric power stations. Every summer, stages are set up along the waterside here for the spectacular **Lent Festival** (see *Nightlife, page 80*).

As you walk, at Vojašniška you will pass the pride of the city, **Stara trta, 8**. This 400-year-old grape vine is the oldest continually producing vine

in the world, and has earned Maribor a place in the *Guinness Book of World Records*. A ceremonial grape harvest takes place each year in September (see *Calendar of Events, page 85*), yielding 35–55kg (77–120lb) of black grapes. These are made into wine at Vinag, and used to fill about 100 artist-designed 25-ml (half-pint) bottles, which are given as protocol gifts to European twin towns and the like. The ancient vine is flanked by younger vines, which were all grown from cuttings.

## The Synagogue

A little way further downriver, on the left at Zidovska 4, you will come to the **Sinagoga** (Synagogue; Mon–Fri 8am–2pm; free). During the Middle Ages, Maribor was home to a large Jewish community that grew wealthy through trading, but members of the community were expelled in the late 15th century and their synagogue was converted into a Roman Catholic

church. By 1785 it was in use as a warehouse, but has now been renovated and become a venue for cultural activities.

The adjoining **Židovski stolp** (Jewish Tower; free) dates back to the late 15th century and is now home to the **Fotogalerija Stolp** (Tower Photography Gallery; Mon–Fri 10am–7pm, Sat 9am–1pm), which mounts changing exhibitions of the work of contemporary Slovenian photographers. Close by, on the riverside, stands the solid, 16th-century **Vodni stolp** (Water Tower), another former defensive structure.

## Maribor Island and the Spa

If you are here between June and September, the most pleasant thing to do is devote the afternoon to a picnic lunch and a swim at **Mariborski Otok** (Maribor Island; daily 9am–8pm; admission fee), 5km (3 miles) west of the old town, close to the village of Kamnica. To get there, either walk or hire a bicycle at the bus station, east of the old town at Mlinksa 1 (tel: 02-235-0212), then follow the riverside promenade, animated by ducks and swans, west of the city centre. On the island, which is accessed by a bridge, there are two swimming pools, grassy areas for sunbathing, and even an area reserved for nudists.

Alternatively, if you are here between May and October, you could have lunch at **Gostišče Pri treh ribnikih** (see *Eating Out, page 76*) in the **City Park** north of the centre, eating outside on a leafy terrace or in vaulted brick cellars, then spend the remainder of the afternoon at the modern **MTC Fontana** (Koroška cesta 172; daily 9am–9pm; admission fee; www.termemb.si), complete with thermal pools, whose water, rich in iodine and fluoride, is kept at a comfortable 33–37ºC (91.4–98.6ºF). There are also whirlpools, a sauna, a solarium, fitness centre and massage services.

**Above:** Maribor roof tops

## 11. PTUJ AND THE JERUZALEM WINE ROAD

**A morning in Ptuj, with its stately hilltop castle, then an afternoon drive along the Jeruzalem *vinska cesta* (wine road), to visit vineyards and cellars and taste some of the country's best white wines.**

*Ptuj can be reached by regular bus services from Maribor, but to follow the wine road you really need private transport. Be sure to telephone in advance if you plan to visit cellars along the way.*

Leave Maribor in the morning, following the main road 25km (15 miles) southeast to **Ptuj**. Built on the right bank of the River Drava, the old town is made up of winding cobbled streets lined by Gothic monuments and baroque mansions, and crowned by a hilltop castle. It was founded by the Romans as Poetovio, and soon developed into an important military, commercial and administrative centre. During the Roman period, some 40,000 people lived in the area – a number never again attained, due to a succession of foreign invasions, floods, fires and epidemics. During the centuries under the Habsburgs, Ptuj and Maribor became commercial rivals, both vying for monopoly over the wine trade with Vienna. Maribor finally gained prominence in 1846 with the opening of its railway link with Vienna.

### The Old Town

The old town centres on **Slovenski trg** (Slovenia Square), home to some of Ptuj's most notable historic buildings. The most striking monument is the **Mestni stolp** (Town Tower) built in 1556, with a clock and an onion dome, which now houses the **Galerija svetli Jurij**

**Above:** old streets in Ptuj
**Right:** Jeruzalem church spire

(St George's Gallery). Around the steps leading up to the entrance, some ancient Roman stones found during excavation are on display.

In front of the Town Tower stands the 5-m (16-ft) high **Orpheus Monument**, a Roman tombstone from the 2nd century, carved with scenes from the story of Orpheus. During the Middle Ages it was used as a 'Pillar of Shame', where local criminals were chained up and exposed to public scorn and ridicule. Behind the Town Tower stands the Gothic **Cerkev svetli Jurji** (Church of St George).

From Slovenski trg follow **Prešernova** past the pink-fronted **Garni Hotel Mitra** (see *Accommodation, page 94*), turn right immediately after **Amadeus gostilna** (No 36), and then right again up a steep cobbled path leading to the castle gate. From here, some 300m (1,000ft) above the town, you have fine views over the terracotta rooftops and the river, across the flat flood plain and beyond with the Pohorje Mountains silhouetted in the distance.

## Ptuj Castle and Regional Museum

**Grad Ptuj** (Ptuj Castle) centres on a baroque courtyard overlooked by three levels of open-arched galleries. Although it dates back to the 12th century, most of what we see today was built between the 15th and 18th centuries, when it was the property of the all-powerful Habsburgs. Since the end of World War II, it has housed the **Ptuj Regional Museum** (summer daily 9am–6pm, until 8pm July–Aug weekends, winter 9am–5pm; admission fee; www.pok-muzej-ptuj.si). The ground floor displays a fine collection of antique musical instruments, including flutes, horns, drums, lutes, violas, harps and clavichords – each cabinet has a motion detector that switches on a record-

**Above Left:** pointing the way to the wine cellars
**Above:** restaurant sign along the wine road

ing of the instruments being played as you walk by. The first floor is devoted to period furniture, while the second floor harbours religious paintings and statues, plus an unusual display of traditional carnival costumes.

During carnival, known here as **Kurentovanje** (see *Calendar of Events, page 84*), local men play the role of *kurenti*, dressing up in sheepskin cloaks with cowbells hung around their waists, their heads covered with hideous masks whose mouths reveal white teeth and a long red tongue. The tradition is rooted in pagan fertility rites, in which the *kurenti* chase away the winter and beckon in the spring.

On leaving the castle, turn left and return to Slovenski trg via the pedestrian **Grajska ulica**. If you are without private transport, have lunch in Ptuj, perhaps at **Ribič** (see *Eating Out, page 76*), which lies at the foot of the old town and serves excellent trout on an open-air terrace overlooking the river. You could then make an afternoon visit to the **Vinska klet** (Wine Cellars; Trsten-jakova 6; tel: 02-787-9810; fee for wine tastings). By prior arrangement, you will be given a tour of the underground cellars along with an audio-visual presentation of the wine-making year, plus a tasting session that offers the chance to sample white wines from the Haloze Hills region, south of Ptuj.

## The Jeruzalem Wine Road

If you have a car, drive 30km (19 miles) from Ptuj to **Ljutomer**, taking the secondary road that passes through **Svetli Tomaž**. There is little to see in Ljutomer itself, its sole peculiarity being the trotting track where horses are trained daily – if you are here on a Sunday afternoon you may catch the fortnightly races. Pick up a Jeruzalem Wine Road map from the Ljutomer Tourist Office at Jureša Cirila 4 (tel: 02-581-1105; www.jeruzalem.si). The wine road runs 18km (11 miles) from Ljutomer to Ormož, criss-crossing a labyrinth of narrow country lanes and passing plenty of vineyards, cellars and restaurants along the way, all of which offer wine-tasting sessions, but you always need to make an appointment. The places mentioned below are in Ivanjkovci and Kog, but you may like to try other options recommended by the Tourist Board.

From Ljutomer, drive 8km (5 miles) south to **Jeruzalem**, a small hilltop village surrounded by undulating hills of lush meadows, vineyards and woodland, and named after the biblical city by the Knights of the Cross who lived here in the 12th century. At the small Tourist Information Centre at Glavni trg 1, you could ask to see a 20-minute audio-visual presentation about the

**Above:** the local grapes

grape harvest, and also buy postcards and souvenirs. From Jeruzalem you can either drive the short distance south to Ivanjkovci, or set off eastwards across country to Kog.

In Ivanjkovci, at Veličane 56, you will find **Zidanica Malek** (daily 11am–6pm; call in advance to organise tastings; tel: 02-741-5725; www.jeruzalem-ormoz.si; fee for tastings). This single-storey white cottage, once belonging to a local count, has been tastefully converted into a wine shop with steps leading down to the vaulted brick cellars. Tasting sessions range from a simple choice of four wines with bread and cheese, to a more elaborate selection that may include *penina* (sparkling wine) and *kasno berba*, a highly-esteemed variety made from late-harvested grapes that have already started to dry and form sugar on their skins.

Some 200m (650ft) beyond Zidanica Malek, on the right, at Veličane 59, lies **Taverna** (tel: 02-7194-128; www.vino-k.de; fee for wine tastings). This restaurant (daily 11am–11pm) serves local dishes in a wooden-beamed dining room with an impressive open stone fireplace (see *Eating Out* and *Accommodation, pages 76 and 95*). Downstairs, the 270-year-old cellars are stocked with oak barrels, where you can taste the wines and, of course, buy bottles to take home.

Alternatively, in Kog, **Hlebec** (Kog 181; tel: 02-713-7060; www.hlebec-kog.net; fee for wine tastings) owns vineyards containing 20,000 grape vines and has been in the Hlebec family for three generations. The owner, Milan Hlebec, is a qualified sommelier and offers wine tasting sessions in the cellars. Šipon, which is the grape most prevalent in this area, is known as Tocai in neighbouring Hungary. It got its local name during the 17th century when French soldiers came to the region, tasted the wine and said '*c'est bon*' which people here quickly mutated to '*šipon*'. If you call in advance, Hlebec can provide lunch or dinner, and they have rooms should you wish to stay the night (see *pages 76 and 94*). Otherwise, if you still feel up to the drive, return to Maribor, passing through Ormož and Ptuj.

*the east*

## 12. ROGAŠKA SLATINA *(see map, page 66)*

A day in Slovenia's oldest and most visited spa town, Rogaška Slatina.
Take the health-giving mineral waters, then have a swim, enjoy a massage, or take part in a relaxation session. Before leaving, check out the
locally-produced crystal.

*Rogaška Slatina can be visited easily as a day trip from Maribor if you
have a car, but public transport is limited; although there is a bus service,
the timetable tends to cut short your stay in the spa town. However, the
town has plenty of hotels, so you could arrange your visit to include an
overnight stay. Health and beauty treatments at the Lotus Wellness Centre
need to be booked in advance. Take the E57 motorway out of Maribor in
the direction of Ljubljana, turn off after 25km (16 miles) at Slovenska Bistrica,
then head south, passing through Poljčane to arrive at Rogaška Slatina, 47km
(29 miles) from Maribor.*

Slovenia has 15 spas, all of which come under
the umbrella of the Slovenian Spas Community (www.spa-slovenia.com). Besides cures
and convalescence, they offer relaxation and
recreation, and the more modern ones also provide a range of health and beauty treatments.
Rogaška Slatina is the country's oldest and
best known spa town, where the Lotus Wellness Centre treats sophisticated visitors to all
the pampering their hearts could desire.

### The Curative Waters

According to local legend, Rogaška Slatina
was founded when the mythical winged-horse
Pegasus, son of Poseidon, god of the sea,
kicked open the mineral springs with his hoof.
The first analysis of the waters was published
in 1572, and the fame of the spring spread
rapidly after 1665 when the Croatian viceroy,
Peter Zrinski, was apparently cured of a debil-
itating illness after taking the waters. From
1803 the village developed into an elegant spa town, patronised by central
Europe's ruling families, including the Habsburgs, the Bourbons and the
Bonapartes. Today it is one of the top spas in central Europe for the treatment
of gastroenterological diseases and metabolic disorders, as well as being a
recreational and beauty resort for those seeking refuge from stress.

Set amid rolling hills of green meadows and woodland, the town is built
around the spa complex, which centres on Zdraviliški trg, a large square with
neatly mown lawns, clipped hedges and formal flower beds, overlooked by
the original 19th-century neoclassical buildings, plus several later, elegant
Secessionist structures and some rather unsightly modernist additions. Many
of the hotels offer one-week packages, which include a consultation, treatment and special diets, attracting Slovenes, visitors from neighbouring Italy,

**Above:** pouring the curative waters in Rogaška Slatina
**Left:** pretty village overlooking the vineyards

Austria and Croatia, plus an increasing
number of travellers from further afield.

On arrival, at the south end of the
square, on the left, you will find a small
Tourist Information Centre (Zdraviliški
trg 1; tel: 03-581-4414) where you can
pick up a plan of the town. From here,
cross the square and walk up the right-
hand side to arrive at the yellow and
white neoclassical **Grand hotel
Rogaška** (Zdraviliški trg 14), originally
built as the *Zdraviliški Dom* (Health
Centre) in 1913. The ground-floor
**Grand Café** makes a perfect spot for
morning coffee.

## Anina Gallery the Tempel

Re-cross the square to check out the
small **Anina galerija** (Zdraviliški trg 4;
Tues–Sun 6–9pm), formerly the
Museum of Graphic Art. It holds a col-
lection of antique etchings and drawings, donated by Kurt Muller, a Swiss
visitor to the resort for many years.

Close by, at the north end of the square, stands the **Tempel**, a small open-
sided neoclassical pavilion built over the Tempel spring in 1819. Directly
behind this lies the public mineral water **Drinking Hall** (daily 7am–1pm,
Mon–Sat also 3–7pm, Sun 4–7pm; fee for glass of water), where you can
sample the range of local waters – Tempel, Styria and Donat – gushing

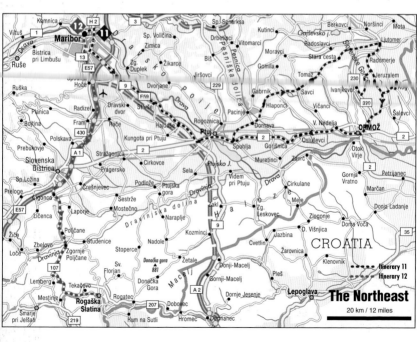

directly from the springs. They may taste rather peculiar, but centuries of experience have proved that at worst they do no harm. Rogaška's best-known water, Donat Mg, is loaded with magnesium – 1 litre (2.1 pints) provides the recommended daily intake of 1,000mg and is claimed to be beneficial for the prevention and treatment of various ailments of the digestive system and metabolism (it is recommended for slimmers), the liver, gall bladder and heart, and to do wonders for psychosomatic disorders. You will find the bottled variety on sale in shops throughout the country, and it is also exported as far afield as Russia.

## Lotus Wellness Centre

To the left of the Tempel, the **Grand hotel Sava** (see *Accommodation, page 95*), connected to the Drinking Hall by a covered passage, offers a special *Ayurvedic* menu, which you might try if you want a healthy lunch. Or, if you have fallen for hearty traditional Slovenian fare, call at **Gostilna Janezov Hram** (see *Eating Out, page 76*) close to the railway station, just a short distance from the centre.

The Grand hotel Sava is home to the extremely sophisticated **Lotus Wellness Centre** (Zdraviliščі trg 6; tel: 03-811-4000; Sun–Thur 7am–8pm, Fri–Sat 7am–11pm; admission fee; www.hotel-sava-rogaska.si), which has been in operation since 2003. You need to make reservations for massage, yoga and hydrotherapy (Mon–Sat 9am–4.30pm, Sun 8.30am–noon; fee per treatment). Here you can seek harmony of mind, body and soul with an ancient Indian Ayurveda massage, join the one-hour stress-relieving *yoga-nidra* session (Mon–Sat 2pm) or try the Atlantis Royal Bath, combining a Jacuzzi-like sensation with aromatherapy, colour therapy and soothing music. Alternatively, spend the afternoon at the central swimming pool where the thermal waters are at a steady 30°C (86°F), and there is a whirlpool with massage jets at 36°C (96.8°F), plus Turkish and Finnish saunas, and a special pool for children.

Before leaving, remember that Rogaška Slatina is renowned for its crystal. The **Steklarna Rogaška Tempel** shop at the south end of the main square (Rogaška Tempel Glassworks; Zdraviliški trg 22; tel: 03-819-0416; Mon–Fri 8am–7pm, Sat 9am–6pm, Sun 9am–1pm) sells a fine selection of drinking glasses, vases and bowls. If you telephone in advance (tel: 03-818-0237), it is possible to arrange a guided tour of the factory (fee), which lies 2km (1 mile) south of town. And if you are here on a summer evening, check the **Rogaška Musical Summer** programme (late June–early Sept). Concerts are held in the **Kristalna dvorana** (Crystal Hall), within the Grand hotel Rogaška, where Hungarian composer and pianist Franz Liszt (1811–86) once performed; and at the Tempel pavilion on the main square.

**Above Left:** Grand Hotel reception area
**Above Right:** bathing in spa waters

# *Leisure Activities*

## SHOPPING

The number of European chain stores that have hit Slovenia's high streets over the last decade is astonishing. The city centres of Ljubljana, Maribor and Koper are now lined with shop fronts featuring the names of large, well-known clothing brands such as Benetton, Sisley, Top Shop and Miss Selfridge. The range of products and their prices are similar to those in other EU countries. At the same time, supermarket culture is gradually creeping into the Slovenian way of life, although fortunately – for the moment at least – many Slovenes remain faithful to their open-air markets for fresh fruit and vegetables and to local vineyards for high-quality wine. These wines, and excellent sports equipment *(see page 71)*, are among the best things to buy in Slovenia.

### Wines

You can buy *vino* (wine) all over the place, but the best and most fun thing is to get it direct from vineyards, wine cellars or agro-tourism centres. While some of these have shops keeping normal opening hours, you normally need to call in advance if you want a full-blown wine-tasting session in the cellars. Tastings generally take you through a selection of four to six wines, beginning with drier varieties and gradually moving towards the sweet, and are accompanied by regional specialities such as cured meats, cheeses and home-made bread. Many of the producers will also pack your purchases in presentation boxes (holding two or three bottles each), which makes them easier to transport and also make fine gifts.

Slovenian quality control and classification are in line with EU regulations. Cheap wines are labelled *namizno vino* (table wine) – drinkable but not outstanding. Next comes *kakovostno vino* (quality wine), and bottles carrying this label have to conform to strict geographical origin rules and can only be made with approved varieties of grapes. An increasing number of excellent wines come under this category, including all sparkling wines made by the tank method and most of the young wines that come onto the market on *Martinovanje* (11 November).

The highest category is *vrhunsko vino* (premium wine), which guarantees strict production methods and grape quality, and prohibits the addition of sugar or acid. Wines are also divided into *suho* (dry), *polsuho* (semi-dry), *polsladko* (semi-sweet) or *sladko* (sweet).

The Slovenian Tourist Board has devised 20 *vinske ceste* (wine roads), passing through the three main wine-making regions: **Primorska**, the coast and Karst area in the southwest; **Podravje**, near the River Drava, including Maribor and Ptuj; and **Posavje**, near the River Sava, east of Ljubljana.

In **Primorska**, red wines predominate. The robust red **Teran** is produced from *refošk* grapes in the 'terracotta' clay soils of the Karst region. The same wine goes under the name of the grape from which it is made, **Refošk**, when produced along the coast. Also near the Adriatic, you'll find the golden-coloured dry white **Malvazija**, often served as house wine in seafood restaurants.

The largest cellar in the Karst region is **Vinakras** (Sejmiška 1; tel: 05-734-1511; Mon–Fri 8am–5pm, Sat 8am–noon, Sun

**Left:** one canoe fits all
**Right:** where to buy the best wine

9am–1pm; www.vinakras.si) in Sežana, while the best-known cellar on the coast is **Vinakoper** (Šmarska 1; tel: 05-663-0100; www.vinakoper.si) in Koper. Both offer tours and wine tasting by prior agreement.

While in the Karst, be sure to look for an *Osmica*, a phenomenon unique to the region. There is no direct translation of the term, but it means literally 'eight days'. The tradition dates back to the mid-18th century, when the Austro-Hungarian Empress, Maria Theresa, passed a law allowing locals a period of eight days to sell the previous year's wine surplus free of tax. It continues to this day, in villages such a Sežana and

Štanjel, where wine makers lay on local specialities such as *pršut* (ham) and *sir* (cheese), cut-price wine, and even music and dancing. For current *Osmica* venues, see www.kras-carso.com/osmice (in Slovenian only).

Slovenia's high-quality white wines are produced in **Podravje** – Renski Rizling, Laški Rizling, Traminec, Sauvignon, Chardonnay, Sivi Pinot (Pinot Gris) and Beli Pinot (Pinot Blanc), plus the sparkling Penina. Most are semi-dry or semi-sweet, although they do not come across as noticeably sweet, as the high levels of acidity balance out the sugar content.

The region's largest outlet is the **Vinag Wine Cellars** *(see page 57)* in Maribor, which produces a good range of whites, and the highly regarded Plenina Royal, a sparkling wine made by the classic champagne process. In neighbouring Ptuj, **Vinska Klet** *(see page 63)* stocks quality whites originating from the Haloze Hills, and there is an audio-visual presentation explaining the process. A short distance south of Maribor, at Slovenska Bistrica (just off the motorway to Ljubljana), **Bistrica Wine Cellar** (Vinarska 3; tel: 02-805-0820; www.klet-bistrica.com) has a capacity of 1 million litres (264,200 gal). All three cellars offer guided tours and wine tasting by appointment.

Close to Ptuj lie two of the top wine producing areas: **Jeruzalem** and **Haloze**. For detailed information about the Jeruzalem Wine Road (see *Itinerary 11*), northeast of Ptuj, contact the **Local Tourist Board Prlekija Ljutomer** (Jureša Cirila 4, Ljutomer; tel: 02-581-1105; www.jeruzalem.si); for more on the Haloze Wine Road, south of Ptuj, try **Halo** (Cirkulane 56, Cirkulane; tel: 02-795-3200; www.halo.si).

The **Posavje** area, which centres on the River Sava but also includes the Krka Valley, is known for the light, sharp, rose-coloured **Cviček**, unique to Slovenia and made from a blend of several red and white varieties. Some scorn it, but it is gradually earning the respect of connoisseurs.

Also worth a mention are two excellent high-class wine-bar-cum-shops in Ljubljana, where you can taste before you buy: one is **Vinoteka GR** at Dunajska 18, north of the centre, inside the Ljubljana trade fair complex; the other is **Movia** at Mestni trg 2 in the heart of the old town. And at Dobrovo, 16km (10 miles) northwest of Nova Gorica, **Vinoteka Brda** (Grajska 10, Dobrovo; tel: 05-395-9210; Tues–Sun 11.30am–9pm; www.vinotekabrda.si), housed in the vaulted brick cellars of the late Renaissance Dobrovo Castle, stocks a vast and tempting selection of wines.

## Markets

Open-air markets are colourful and entertaining, with beautifully arranged stalls selling locally grown seasonal fruit and vegetables in the early morning and closing with a chaotic clean-up in the afternoon. There has been a rise in imported fruit and vegetables, which will continue to increase now Slovenia is in the EU, but the two words to keep in mind when shopping for fresh produce remain 'regional' and 'seasonal'. Wherever you go, the largest and busiest markets are held on Saturday.

**Above:** buying flowers from a market stall

Ljubljana's fruit and vegetable market (Mon–Sat 7am–3pm) takes place on Vodnikov trg next to the cathedral, alongside Tržnica, the riverside colonnade housing bakers' kiosks at ground level, and spiral stairs leading down to the meat and fish stalls inside. The **Ljubljana Flea Market** (Sun 8am–1pm) on Cankarjevo nabrežje – the river bank close to the Triple Bridge – sells everything from genuine antiques to Yugoslav military gear. The market in **Maribor** (Mon–Sat 7am–2pm) is on Vodikov trg in the old town close to the river. A more rough-and-ready affair, its stalls are laden with everything from fruit and vegetables to home-made wine and dairy produce, plus household items and clothes. **Koper**'s market (Mon–Sat 7am–2pm) is at Tržnica, just off Pristaniška between the old town and the sea, with fruit and vegetable stalls outside and meat and fish in a covered hall.

## Sports Equipment

With skiing and hiking topping the national leisure activities, Slovenia is home to two manufacturers of high-quality sports equipment. **Elan** (www.elansports.com), with its main factory in Begunje na Gorenjskem, near Lake Bled, make skis and snowboards. The company, founded as a co-operative in 1945, produces some 400,000 pairs of skis per annum, 80 percent for export – more than 15 million pairs over the years. It has gained universal respect for its technical innovation. **Planika** (www.planika.si) is the other company, and it makes hiking and mountaineering boots. Based in Kranj, it was founded in 1951 (in the days of the former Yugoslavia) and is now also exporting to other European countries. You will find both Elan and Planika products available in good sports shops throughout the country.

## Souvenirs

A bottle of potent žganju will bring back memories of the bars and restaurants you visited during your stay in Slovenia. You can buy commercially produced varieties in most supermarkets, but some of the best comes from **Pleterje Monastery** in the Krka Valley (see *Itinerary 2*). The monks make their own *viljamovka* (with a whole pear inside the bottle) and *slivovka* (based on plums), both sold at the monastery shop. Some agrotourism centres sell their own home brews.

Slovenia has a long tradition of **honey** production – in the 18th century, a Slovene named Anton Janša became a world-respected authority on bee-keeping. You can buy honey at **Stična Monastery** in the Krka Valley, at Pleterje, and at some markets – in Ljubljana's open-air market honey is sold in hand-painted jars. The Stična Monastery shop also sells a selection of Father Simon Ašič's **herbal teas**, each one said to cure a specific ailment such as insomnia, poor memory or even cellulite. Alternatively, the best-known Slovenian brand name in herbal teas is **Droga**; their packaged teas are available in shops throughout the country.

The mining town of Idrija (see *Itinerary 7*) is packed with small craft shops selling local hand-made **lace**. For some of the most original designs, call at **Studio Irma Vončina** on the main square (Mestni trg 17; tel: 05-377-1584; Mon–Fri 10am–noon, 1–4pm, Sat 10am–noon).

Last, but not least, the spa town of Rogaška Slatina (see *Itinerary 12*) is known for **crystal**. The **Steklarna Rogaška Tempel** shop on the main square (Zdravliški trg 22; tel: 03-819-0416; Mon–Fri 8am–7pm, Sat 9am–6pm, Sun 9am–1pm) sells glasses, vases and bowls. If you telephone in advance, it is also possible to arrange a guided tour of the factory (tel: 03-818-0170; www.steklarna-rogaska.si), a few kilometres outside the town.

**Right:** Ljubljana's Central Market

## EATING OUT

Eastern and Central European food has a reputation for being bland and stodgy, but you will soon discover that you can eat extremely well here. The nation's cuisine has been heavily influenced by the neighbouring countries that have at one time occupied its territory – Austria, Hungary

and Italy – resulting in a wide variety of regional specialities. In the northeast you can expect *Dunajski zrezek* (Wiener schnitzel) and *gulaž* (goulash) from Austria and Hungary respectively, while in the southwest you will feast upon Italian-inspired *pršut* (cured ham, similar to *prosciutto*) and *rižota* (risotto).

### What to Eat

To get a taste of honest, down-to-earth Slovenian fare, eat at a *gostilna* (tavern), where you can expect a range of hearty staples such as *jota* (a heavy soup of beans, sauerkraut and barley), *krvavica* (black pudding) served with *žganci* (polenta), *klobasa* (sausage) with *kislo zelje* (sauerkraut), plus the much-loved *štruklji* (dumplings), both sweet and savoury.

For more refined dining, go to a *restavracija* (restaurant), where service is more formal and the menu will feature such expensive main courses as *mešeno meso na*

*žaru* (mixed platter of barbecued meats) and *riba na žaru* (barbecued fresh fish). Look out for subtle seasonal and regional treats such as *tartufi* (truffles, served with either pasta or steak), *postrv* (trout – the best come from the River Soča and Lake Bohinj), and colourful salads made from *rukola* (rocket) and the bitter-sweet purple radicchio.

Regarding snacks, although Slovenians are adamant that theirs is a 'Western' culture, they have maintained a truly Balkan susceptibility for Turkish-inspired *burek* (filo pastry filled with either curd cheese or minced meat) and *čevapčiči* (kebabs), both of which are sold at street kiosks in all the larger towns and resorts.

If you have a sweet tooth, head for a *slaščičarna* (cake shop) or a high-class *kavarna* (café). Here you can indulge in *potica*, a sweet roll filled with walnuts or poppy seeds, and the irresistible *prekmurska gibanica*, a delicious calorie-laden cake made up of layers of filo pastry, cream cheese, poppy seeds, walnuts and apple. Other standard deserts are *palačinke* (pancakes, filled with either apricot jam, ground walnuts or chocolate) and *sladoled* (ice cream).

Restaurants and taverns aside, to taste the most authentic local specialities, eat at a *turist kmetija* (agrotourism centre), where most of the dishes on offer will be made from home produce, in some cases organic.

### What to Drink

Slovenians generally order *vino* (wine) with their meals, or in some cases *pivo* (beer). Quality wines (see Shopping, pages 68–70) to look out for are the red Teran from the Karst area and a range of whites (Rizling, Traminec, Sauvignon, Chardonnay, Pinot Blanc and Pinot Noir) from the northeast. The top beers are Laško Zlatorog and Union. Many people ask for a bottle of *mineralna voda* (mineral water) at the table, while *sok* (fruit juice) is a popular option for children.

To fit in with current working trends, Slovenians generally eat their main meal in the evening, and just have a snack for lunch. Opening hours vary from region to region and season to season. Taverns are generally open from early morning to mid-evening, serving drinks and meals throughout the day, and they often have a 'menu of the day' that

**Above:** a plate of cured ham accompanied by Teran wine

usually represents excellent value for money (not something you will find in the more sophisticated restaurants). Some restaurants open for dinner only; those in the mountains tend to close early (in Bohinj most are shut by 10pm), while those along the coast may stay open well into the small hours, at least during July and August.

## Where to Eat

The prices below are based on an average meal for two, with house wine:

€       under €30
€€      €30–60
€€€     over €60

## Ljubljana

### AS

*Čopov 5a (off Knafljev prehod)*
*Tel: 01-425-8822*
Considered by many to be the best restaurant in town, AS is renowned for its outstanding seafood dishes and superior wine list. Intimate cosy interior with antique furniture. Reservations recommended. €€€

### Pri Škofu

*Rečna 8, Krakovo*
*Tel: 01-426-4508*
Located in the Krakovo district, a 10-minute walk south of the city centre, this colourful, bohemian-style eatery serves up creative Slovenian cuisine concocted from fresh, seasonal produce from the local open-air market. Open daily. €€

### Ribca

*Glavna Tržnica (Central Market)*
*No phone*
In an open-sided arcade looking onto the River Ljubljanica, Ribca serves freshly fried fish (sardines, whitebait, squid) plus salads. Great place for lunch. Open Mon–Fri 7am–4pm, Sat 8am–2pm. €

### Sokol

*Ciril Metodov trg 18*
*Tel: 01-439-6855*
*www.gostilna-sokol.com*
Hearty traditional soups and roast meat dishes served in a series of rustic wooden dining rooms on several levels. Round off

with delicious *prekmurska gibanica* for dessert. Popular with local people for lunch rather than dinner. €€

### Špajza

*Gornji trg 28*
*Tel: 01-425-3094*
A series of small rooms with Bohemian decor and candles set a romantic atmosphere. The chef produces creative Mediterranean dishes such as risotto with porcini mushrooms and colourful fresh salads of rocket and radicchio. €€€

### Zlata ribica

*Cankarjevo nabrežje 5*
*Tel: 01-426-9490*
Close to the Triple Bridge, this old favourite, serving Slovenian dishes with an Italian twist, has a sleek mustard-yellow and burgundy-red interior. It's heaving on Sunday lunchtimes when the antiques market takes place outside. €€

## Krka Valley

### Hotel Grad Otočec

*Grajska 2, Otočec*
*Tel: 07-384-8600*
*www.terme-krka.si*
The restaurant of this 13th-century castle hotel, 8km (5 miles) west of Šentjernej on the road to Novo Mesto, features game as the house speciality. Meals are served in a wooden-beamed dining room with an open fireplace. Alternatively, you could just stop off for a drink in the pleasant courtyard café. €€€

**Right:** al fresco eating in the capital

### Šeruga

*Sela pri Ratežu 15, Otočec*
*Tel: 07-334-6900*
*www.seruga.si*
Agrotourism centre, 10km (6 miles) from Novo Mesto. Specialities include rabbit, trout, and *štruklji* (dumplings), plus home-made *Cviček* wine. Reservations essential. €€

## Bled

### Gostilna Pri Planincu

*Grajska 8*
*Tel: 04-574-1613*
Established in 1903, this tavern is as popular today as ever. Serves generous portions of home-made country fare in a pub-like ambience, plus pizzas in the back garden. Locals love it, and so do most visitors. €€

### Mlino

*Cesta svobode 45.*
*Tel: 04-574-1404*
*www.mlino.si*
A 15-minute walk from the centre brings you to this popular restaurant, on the main road next to the lake. There are boat trips to the island from the landing stage out front. €€

### Zaka

*Župančičeva 9*
*Tel: 04-574-1709*
*www.bled-zaka.com*
A 30-minute walk from town along the lakeside brings you to this waterfront restaurant close to the public bathing area. It serves a good choice of traditional dishes. €€

## Bohinj

### Erlah

*Ukanc 67*
*Tel: 04-572-3309*
At the west end of the lake, close to Hotel Zlatorog, Erlah has long been a favourite lunch spot for hikers. Serve fresh *postrv* (trout), *palačinke* (pancakes) and *štrukli* (dumplings filled with cheese or walnuts) on an open-air terrace. €€

### Gostilna Mihovc

*Stara Fužina 118*
*Tel: 04-572-3390*
A village tavern, popular with hikers, serving down-to-earth home-cooking, including *jota* (heavy soup of beans and sauerkraut). Ask for *palačinke* (pancakes) if you fancy something sweet. €

### Planinska Koča Merjasec

*Mt Vogel*
*No phone*
Close to the Vogel Ski Centre at the upper stop of the cable car, this Alpine mountain hut is open all year to serve hearty dishes to hikers or skiers, depending on the season. The house speciality is wild boar. €€

### Zlatovčica

*Hotel Jezero, Ribčev Laz 51*
*Tel: 04-572-9100*
This hotel restaurant takes its name from the delicious Bohinj golden trout that feature on the menu. It's on an open terrace, a 5-minute walk from Lake Bohinj. €€

## Soča Valley/Kobarid

### Topli Val

*Hotel Hvala, Trg Svobode 1, Kobarid*
*Tel: 05-389-9300*
*www.topli-val-sp.si*
This hotel restaurant serves some of the country's best seafood, despite its inland location, and is popular with Italians, who cross the border especially to eat here. €€€

## Piran and Portorož

### Barka

*Svobode 3, Piran*
*No phone*
Down-to-earth place serving Balkan-style fast food: *čevapčiči* (kebabs), burgers, sausages and chips. Take away, or eat at the wooden tables and benches inside. €

### Cantina

*Trg 1 Maja 10, Piran*
*Tel: 05-673-3275*

**Left:** a waiter at work in the Topli Val restaurant, Kobarid

With rustic wooden tables overlooking the square, this is a great place to try the local *refošk* wine, along with platters of *pršut* (prosciutto ham), cheese and olives. **€€**

## Gostilna Korte

*Korte 44, Korte, Portorož*
*Tel: 05-642-0200*

A long-standing institution, the Gostilna Korte tavern is renowned throughout the country. In a small village amid vineyards in the hills behind Portorož, it serves local specialities along with home-made *Refošk* wine. Open daily noon–midnight. **€€**

## Neptun

*Župančičeva 7, Piran*
*Tel: 05-673-4111*

Situated in the heart of the old town, the friendly Neptun serves top-quality seafood, as well as meat, pasta, risotto and truffle dishes. It has a small dining room, as well as tables out on the pedestrianised side street. Local people claim it is the best restaurant in town. **€€€**

## Ribič

*Seča 143, Portorož*
*Tel: 05-677-0790*

About 1.5km (1 mile) from the centre of Portorož, Ribič has a deservedly good reputation for quality seafood dishes served in a pleasant garden overlooking the salt pans. Open Wed–Mon. **€€€**

## Verdi

*Verdijeva 18, Piran*
*Tel: 05-673-2737*

Also in the old town, between Tartinijev trg and Trg 1 Maja, Verdi serves exquisite seafood on its large open-air terrace. The service is professional but rather formal. Open Thur–Tues. **€€€**

# Idrija and Nova Gorica

## Gurman

*Gradnikove brigade 51, Nova Gorica*
*Tel: 05-302-1941*

Tasty traditional seafood and meat dishes are served on the open-air terrace in summer, and in the wooden-floored dining room throughout the winter months. Open Mon–Fri and Sat evenings. **€€**

## Restauracija Barbara

*Kosovelova 3, Idrija*
*Tel: 05-377-1162*

Just a five-minute walk from the Idrija Mercury Mine, this is the place to try such Idrijan specialities as *žlikrofi* (potato balls flavoured with marjoram and wrapped in fine dough), *zeljševka* (rolled yeast dough with herb filling) and *smukavc* (cabbage soup with potatoes). Open Mon–Fri 4–10pm. **€€€**

# The Karst

## Gombač

*Lokev 165, Lokev*
*Tel: 05-767-0466*

Situated on the road to Lipica Stud Farm, this local eatery serves genuine and tasty Karst fare, including succulent roast lamb, rabbit and radicchio with beans. Open Thur–Tues. **€€**

## Jamska

*Jamska 30, Postojna Cave*
*Tel: 05-700-0103*

Situated at the entrance to Postojna Cave, this restaurant, serving the usual range of Slovenian fare, is highly-regarded locally, but it often gets filled up with coach parties, so is not the place to come for a peaceful meal. **€€**

**Above:** the robust red Teran wine from Primorska

## Koper

### Istrska klet
*Župančičeva 39, Koper*
*Tel: 05-627-6729*
Tiny, no-frills wine bar with plenty of charm, and popular with local fishermen. Only two or three tables, but it serves delicious *njoki* (gnocchi) and *bakala* (salt-cod). Open Sun–Fri 8am–10pm. €

### Skipper
*Kopališko nabrežje 3, Koper*
*Tel: 05-626-1810*
Overlooking the yachting marina, Skipper is popular with the sailing fraternity. Dine on meat, fish, pasta and risotto dishes on the rooftop terrace with a sea view. €€€

### Za gradom
*Kraljeva 10, Koper*
*Tel: 05-628-5505*
Sophisticated dishes prepared from local, seasonal produce are served here. It's located 1.5km (1mile) outside the city centre, on Semedela Hill. Reservations are essential. Open Tues–Sat. €€€

## Maribor

### Gostilna Pri treh ribnikih
*Ribniska 9*
*Tel: 02-234-4170*
In operation for some 300 years, this restaurant lies in the City Park, next to the three fish ponds from which it takes its name. You can eat outside on a leafy terrace, or in the impressive vaulted brick cellars. €€

### Toti rotovž
*Glavni trg 14*
*Tel: 02-228-7650*
In the 16th-century Town Hall building, this restaurant serves a decent range of Slovenian dishes on the ground-floor level, while barbecued steaks are the speciality in the vaulted brick cellars. €€

### Restauracija Marina
*Limbuško nabrežje 2*
*Tel: 02-420-0750*
*www.marina-mb.com/gb*
Located on the River Drava, about 3km (2 miles) west of Maribor, Marina serves a good choice of freshwater fish, as well as roast meats, gnocchi and pasta dishes. €€

## Ptuj and the Jeruzalem Wine Road

### Ribič
*Dravska ulica 9, Ptuj*
*Tel: 02-749-0635*
*www.gostilna-ribic.si*
With a terrace giving onto the river, the specialities here are *ribji brodet* (fish stew) and *postrv* (trout). It's probably the best restaurant in Ptuj. Open Tues–Sun. €€

### Hlebec
*Kog 108, Kog*
*Tel: 02-713-7060*
This is a wine cellar that serves delicious local specialities, such as cream of mushroom soup. *pogača* (cheese pie), roast meats and home-made sausages, along with some of the country's finest wines. Reservations are essential. €€

### Taverna
*Svetinje 21, Ivanjkovci*
*Tel: 02-719-4128*
*www.taverna-jeruzalem.si*
The Taverna serves fresh trout and platters of roast meats in an old-fashioned dining room that commands a fantastic hilltop view over the surrounding vineyards and woodlands. Occasional live music. €€

## Rogaška Slatina

### Gostilna Janezov hram
*Kidričeva 44*
*Tel: 03-581-3957*
This tavern serves a wide range of Slovenian fare, including venison, along with home-baked bread and their own wine. You can eat on an open-air terrace throughout the summer. €€

**Left:** fresh seafood that looks as good as it tastes

# NIGHTLIFE

Ljubljana is the main hub of see-and-be-seen bars, glitzy nightclubs, high-brow cultural entertainment and alternative venues, thanks largely to its vast student population – there are about 50,000 university and college students, who make up 15 percent of the total population. The city buzzes throughout the year, although in summer many of the students disappear, and the nightlife becomes more low-key, with sedate evening promenades and open-air performances taking over from the late-night winter clubbing scene. Maribor lies in second place in the nightlife stakes, with a limited number of nightspots, but a reputation for excellent wine and a local population with a noteworthy drinking capacity. Along the coast you find bars with summer terraces for an evening drink beneath the stars, open-air cultural entertainment and Slovenia's largest nightclub, strategically located near the sea. In the mountains, forget late-night activities because many restaurants and bars shut at 10pm – unless you are at one of the ski resorts, such as Kranjska Gora, in season.

The bars, nightclubs, theatres and casinos listed here are accessible from places featured in the itineraries.

## Ljubljana

Café life centres on the riverside promenades and the nearby squares in the old town, while cultural entertainment and nightclubs are concentrated in the area between the river and the railway station. For listings, see the tri-monthly English-language *Ljubljana Life*, available free from hotels and tourist offices.

## Bars and Cafés
### Café Galerija
*Mestni trg 5*
A cool, up-market bar close to the Town Hall, with an ornate, Turkish-style interior, funky music and excellent cocktails.

### Maček
*Krojška 5*
The trendiest Ljubljana café, with tables outside overlooking the river in summer. Also buzzing on Sunday morning when the Ljubljana Flea Market takes place close by.

### Movia
*Mestni trg 2*
Sophisticated wine bar and shop with quality Slovenian wines, ideal for an aperitif.

### AS Lounge
*Knafljev prehod 5a*
Unlike the smart restaurant upstairs (see *page 73*), this popular bar has a rowdy, pub-like atmosphere with a DJ and dance floor, and an open-air terrace in summer.

### Gajo Jazz Bar
*Beethovnova 8*
*www.jazzclubgajo.com*
Highly-regarded jazz bar with regular live concerts. When no one playing, it's laid-back and friendly, a great place for a drink to a low-key background of taped trad jazz.

### Saloon
*Trubarjeva 23*
A short walk east of Prešeren Square, Saloon has a 1970s-style leopard-skin and velvet interior and chill out music.

### Orto
*Grablovičeva 1*
Hard-core live music – rock, punk, blues and trash metal. International names on stage upstairs, a hard drinking, smoky bar below. East of the station, near Metelkova.

**Right:** modern décor in a Stari trg café, Ljubljana

### Nightclubs
#### Global
*Tomišičeva 1*
*Tel: 01-426-9020*
*www.global.si*
Global opened in 2004 to instant success, leading many people to proclaim it the hippest club in town. It's situated on the sixth floor of the Nama building, accessed via a glass lift, and has a large terrace with stunning views of floodlit Ljubljana Castle, and a dance floor with predominantly disco and house music. There's even a cash point conveniently placed beside the bar, just in case you run out of money.

#### Bachus
*Kongresni Trg 3*
*Tel: 01-241-8244*
*www.bachus-center.com*
The main rival to Global, with a labyrinth of spaces on several levels. A dance floor with a giant video screen, a café, lounge, pool hall, and assorted bars.

#### Klub SubSub
*Celovška 25*
*www.subsub.si*
Claiming to be the oldest club in Ljubljana, SubSub hosts an assortment of nights with the emphasis on great music – including hip hop, reggae, funk and breakbeat.

### Culture
#### Cankarjev Dom
*Trg republike*
*Tel: 01-241-7299/7300*
*www.cd-cc.si*
Modern arts and convention centre, with 13 performance spaces hosting cultural events ranging from classical to popular music, dance performances, art exhibitions and film screenings.

#### Slovenska Filharmonija
*Kongresni trg 10*
*Tel: 01-241-0800*
*www.filharmonija.si*
The Philharmonic Hall is home to the Slovenian Philharmonic Orchestra and Ljubljana's foremost classical music venue.

#### Kinoteka
*Miklošičeva 28*
*Tel: 01-434-2520*
*www.kinoteka.si*
Arts cinema showing cult classics, retrospectives and premières. On most evenings there are three films (original version, with Slovenian sub-titles), generally starting at 6pm, 8pm and 10pm.

### Alternative Youth Scene
#### Metelkova
*Metelkova (behind Celica Youth Hostel)*
*www.metelkova.org*
An independent cultural centre in a former army barracks, its most popular spot being Klub Gromka, with a bar, mellow world music, and occasional live concerts and happenings. A kitchen serves freshly-made chicken, falafel and kebabs. Programme information is scanty – the only way to find out what's on can be to go and see.

#### Klub K4
*Kersnikova 4*
*www.klubk4.org*
A student-run nightclub leading the city's alternative scene since the 1980s, with music ranging from rock to jazz, folk to hip hop. Also look out for techno parties, performance art and even travel lectures. Open during university term time only.

### Maribor
#### Bars
#### Kavarna Astoria
*Slovenska 2*
Green-fronted café on the edge of Grajski trg (Town Square), for decades a favourite

**Above:** dancing the night away at Global nightclub

local meeting place. Closes early (10pm) but a perfect spot for an early evening drink.

### Patrick's J&B Pub
*Poštna 10*
*Between Glavni trg and Slomski trg*
An Irish pub serving a wide range of draught beers, imported bottled beers, whiskies, cocktails and even Irish coffee. It is extremely popular, especially on Friday and Saturday evening.

### Takos
*Mesarski prehod 3*
*Tel: 02-252-7150*
Mexican restaurant close to the river, serving meals all day and transforming into a club at night. With an emphasis on such Mexican drinks as Tequila, Sol beer and Dos Equis XX lager, it's popular with local people and tourists alike, and there are tables outside during summer. Open till late.

## Clubs
### Jazz Klub Satchmo
*Strossmayerjeva 6*
*Tel: 02-250-2150*
*www.jazz-klub.si*
Located in the cellars below the art gallery, Satchmo plays mainly jazz, with occasional rhythm-and-blues, soul, and funk concerts. Open till late.

## Culture
### Letni Kino
*Grajski trg*
This is an open-air summer cinema situated in the old town.

## Piran
## Bars and Cafés
Bars in the old town centre of Piran tend to close at midnight, so if you want to dance the night away, head for Portorož.

### Café Teater
*Stjenkova 1*
This is Piran's trendiest café-bar, next door to the yellow Tartini Theatre, with an Irish pub-style interior décor and a large summer terrace overlooking the harbour. Open throughout the day, every day, for coffee,

cakes and a wide range of drinks, including imported beers. Occasional live music.

### Cantina Zizola
*Tartinijev trg 10*
A tiny bar hidden away on the corner of Tartinjev trg, with several tables outside where you can order a glass of local wine and contemplate Piran's stunning main square.

### Punta Bar
*Prešernova 24*
Located close to Punta, the tip of the peninsula upon which the old town is built, with tables outside overlooking the sea. The good music attracts a young, alternative crowd.

## Portorož
## Clubs
Portorož has many clubs, particularly along the Obala promenade, and they tend to have a slightly sleazy feel.

### Paprika
*Obala 20a*
*Tel: 05-674-8264*
One of the best clubs in Portorož with an ultra-modern interior hosting a variety of music nights with local and visiting DJs. It functions as a café during the day.

## Koper
## Bars
### Loggia Café
*Titov trg 1*
Located in the 17th-century Venetian loggia overlooking Koper's beautiful main square, the Loggia is the best place in town for a pre-dinner aperitif or a whisky nightcap after a night on the town.

## Casinos
Slovenia has established itself as something of a gambling centre, probably due to the fact that casinos are banned in most parts of Italy, and Italians are happy to hop over the border to indulge in a game of chance.

**Right:** a sunny sign in the Loggia Café, Koper

**Casino Portorož**
*Obala 75A, Portorož*
*Tel: 05-676-0373*
*www.casino.si*
With a capacity of up to 6,000, the casino is divided into two principal areas – the classic games salon, offering Caribbean poker, blackjack, American roulette, French roulette, trente et quarante, chemin de fer, punto banco and seven stud card poker, plus a more informal salon with some 300 slot machines.

**Casino Perla**
*Kidričeva 7, Nova Gorica*
*Tel: 05-336-4000*
*www.hit.si*
This is one of the largest casinos in Europe, with 43 gaming tables (including 28 American roulette tables and 12 blackjack tables) plus a staggering 800 slot machines. Open 24 hours every day.

## Summer Festivals
**Ljubljana – Druga Godba**
*Tel: 01-430-8260*
*www.drugagodba.si*
A one-week festival of alternative and world music (Druga Godba simply means 'other music'). It is held in late May, with events taking place in the Križanke Theatre, Klub K4, and on streets around the town, and has been an annual event since 1984.

**Ljubljana Festival**
*Tel: 01-241-6000*
*www.ljubljanafestival.si*
Open-air concerts, opera, dance and theatre performances at Križanke Theatre, Ljubljana Castle, and various other venues in the city centre, from June to mid-September. This has been an annual event since 1953, with internationally known past performers including Yehudi Menuhin, José Carreras, Wynton Marsalis, and the Bolshoi Theatre from Moscow.

**Ljubljana Jazz Festival**
*Tel: 01-241-7100*
*www.ljubljanajazz.si*
A week-long jazz festival held at Cankarjev Dom in early June. This popular event has been running for more than 50 years.

**Maribor – Lent Festival**
*Tel: 02-234-6611*
*www.maribor-pohorje.si*
This is a three-week festival running from late June into early July, always scheduled to begin on the first Friday after mid-summer's longest day (21 June). Stages are set up along the riverside promenade, known as Lent, on the edge of the old town. An eclectic range of events includes folk dancing, ballet, classical music, pop, world music, rock, and jazz. There's a firework display on the closing evening. Past performers include huge names such as Ray Charles, BB King and James Brown.

**Rock Otočec**
*Tel: no phone*
*www.rock-otocec.com*
Slovenia's biggest annual rock festival takes place in the grounds of Otočec Castle in the Krka Valley in early July. Past performers at the three-day bonanza include Fun Lovin' Criminals and Asian Dub Foundation, as well as many underground bands from the countries of former Yugoslavia.

**Tartini Festival**
*Tel: 031-419-016 (mobile)*
*www.tartinifestival.org*
Each summer, from mid-August to mid-September, Piran celebrates the works of its best-known son, the 18th-century violinist and composer, Giuseppe Tartini, with a festival of classical music.

**Bled International Music Festival**
*Tel: 04-531-7610*
*www.festivalbled.com*
This is a two-week festival held from late June into early July, and staged at various venues in Bled and the surrounding area. It attracts both Slovenian and international violinists. During the same period there are competitions, and master classes are offered by internationally acclaimed teachers.

**Above**: a casino welcomes punters

## Sports And Outdoor Activities

Slovenia's countryside offers plenty of opportunities for sports and outdoor activities, bolstered by the resident population's enthusiasm for them, particularly for skiing and hiking.

### Beaches

Slovenia has a coastline of just 47km (29 miles), and most Slovenians prefer to go to Croatia when it comes to spending time on the beach. However, Portorož has a beach area (of imported sand) with sun-beds and umbrellas for hire, and Bernadin, between Portorož and Piran, has a concrete 'beach' with easy access to the water. The best natural beaches lie between Piran and Fiesa, and at Strunjan, just north of Fiesa.

Naturism began in Yugoslavia in the early 20th century, and nude bathing remains popular in Slovenia today. You'll find areas reserved for nudists at Strunjan on the coast, and inland on Maribor Island (see *Itinerary 10*) on the River Drava.

### Canoeing, Kayaking and Rafting

The falls and rapids of the River Soča (see *Itinerary 5*) and its tributaries are among the most beautiful and challenging in Europe for kayaking, canoeing and white-water rafting. The best points of departure are Kobarid or Bovec: **X-Point** (Stresova 1, Kobarid; tel: 05-388-5308; www.xpoint.si) and **Soča Rafting** (Trg golobarskih žrtev 14, Bovec; tel: 05-389-6200; www.socarafting.si) can arrange training and tours with expert guides, and also provide the necessary equipment.

The River Krka (see *Itinerary 2*) is also good, although more gentle. **K2M** (Pionirska cesta 3, Dolenjska Toplice; tel: 07-306-6830; www.k2m.si) can organise canoeing, kayaking and rafting tours.

On Lake Bohinj (see *Itinerary 4*), **Alpinsport** (Ribčev laz 53; tel: 04-572-3486; www.alpinsport.si) rent kayaks and rowing boats, which make a great way to explore the lake and the surrounding shores.

### Caving and Potholing

There are some 4,000 caves in Slovenia, several of which are artificially lit and open to tourists, the best known being Postojna (see *Itinerary 8*) in the Karst region. More adventurous visitors may like to explore the lesser known caves, and sports agencies such as **3 glav Adventures** (Ljubljanska 1, Bled; mobile tel: 041-683-184; www.3glav-adventures.com) can arrange caving and potholing tours with qualified guides.

### Climbing

The main area for climbing lies within Triglav National Park in the northwest of the country, where a series of routes leading up Mt Triglav's north face present the biggest challenge. **3 glav Adventures** *(see above for details)* and **Julijana Turizem** (Borovška 61, Kranjska Gora; tel: 04-588-1326; www.sednjek.si) specialise in the Julian Alps area, and can organise Alpine climbing trips within Triglav National Park.

### Cycling

Slovenia's varied topography, from the rugged mountains of Triglav National Park to the flat flood plains of the northeast, offers many challenges to cyclists. There is a network of well-maintained cycling trails of varying lengths and difficulty, some of which can be combined with rail transport (bicycles travel free of charge in the luggage com-

**Right:** setting off for a spot of white-water rafting

partments of Intercity and regional trains). Local tourist information centres can supply cycling maps and recommend services such as accommodation en route.

In the mountainous northwest, you can hire mountain bikes from **Alpinsport** (Ribčev laz 53; tel: 04-572-3486; www.alpinsport.si) in Bohinj. Close by, in the Soča Valley, **X-Point** (Stresova 1, Kobarid; tel: 05-388-5308; www.xpoint.si) organise mountain biking tours, although they do not rent bikes to individuals. Also, in 2004, a Bicycle Park, with bikes for hire, opened in Kranjska Gora (www.kranjska-gora.si). The 2km (1-mile) course, suitable for beginners as well as more experienced cyclists, has a downhill run with a 310-m (1,017-ft) descent and 25 obstacles.

In Ljubljana and Maribor there are specially dedicated bike lanes. You can hire bikes in Ljubljana at the **Railway Station** (Trg OF), and in Maribor at the **Bus Station** (Mlinska 1). In Piran, you can hire bicycles from **News Café Bernadin** (Obala 41; tel: 05-674-1004) and **Atlas Express** (Obala 55; tel: 05-674-6772).

### Fishing
Slovenia's fast-flowing rivers and pristine mountain lakes offer clean, well-stocked waters. Fishing enthusiasts consider the River Soča (see *Itinerary 5*) to be one of the top places in Europe for trout and grayling. Kobarid makes an ideal base, and you can obtain fishing permits from Hotel Hvala (Trg Svobode 1, Kobarid; tel: 05-389-9300; www.topli-val-sp.si). The season runs from April to the end of October.

### Golf
Set amid stunning mountain scenery, the 18-hole King Course at **Bled Golf and Country Club** (Kidričeva 10; tel: 04-537-7711; www.golfbled.com), 3km (2 miles) east of Lake Bled (see *Itinerary 3*), is one of most beautiful courses in Europe. Constructed in 1938, it is the best and oldest golf course in Slovenia. There is also an 18-hole course, overlooked by a splendid medieval castle, at **Hotel Golf Grad Mokrice** (www.termecatez.si) in the Krka Valley (see *Itinerary 2*), and a new 18-hole course, close to the stud farm at **Lipica** (www.lipica.org) in the Karst region. These two courses were laid out by the internationally renowned golf course designer, Donald Harradine. You will also find an 18-hole course at **Ptuj** (www.golfptuj.com, see *Itinerary 11*) in the northeast of the country.

### Hiking
Slovenes love their mountains, and hiking is the second most popular sport after skiing. The **Planinska Zveza Slovenija** (Alpine Association of Slovenia, Dvoržakova 9, Ljubljana; tel: 01-434-5680; www.pzs.si) can supply detailed information about the country's 7,000km (4,375 miles) of hiking trails – marked with a white circle within a red circle – and 165 mountain huts. The hiking season in the mountains runs between April and November.

The most spectacular Alpine scenery lies within the confines of Triglav National Park, where **3 glav Adventures** (*see previous page for details*) can arrange anything from a few hours of gentle walking to the chance of tackling Slovenia's highest peak, Mt Triglav. Likewise, the Bohinj-based adventure sports agency **Alpinsport** (Ribčev laz 53; tel: 04-572-3486; www.alpinsport.si) organises group hiking tours of the surrounding area. From Bohinj, it's also possible to do a two-day hike to Kobarid (see *Itinerary 5*) organised by **X-Point** (Stresova 1, Kobarid; tel: 05-388-5308; www.xpoint.si).

**Above:** fly-fishing in the river

If you wish to plan your own hiking itinerary with Triglav NP, *Walking in the Julian Alps* by Simon Brown (see *Practical Information: Further Reading*) is a useful reference guide. It divides the region into four areas, centring on Bled, Bohinj, Kranjska Gora and Bovec, and suggests a selection of routes of varying difficulty from each.

Inexperienced walkers can enjoy easy routes such as the circuits around the lakes of Bled and Bohinj, or theme trails such as the Kobarid Historic Walk. At the opposite end of the scale, serious hikers might be tempted to tackle the Slovenian Alpine Trail, which crosses the country from Maribor in the northeast to Ankaran on the coast, taking in the country's highest peaks en route, or to walk sections of the E6 and E7 European Hiking Trails, both of which pass through Slovenia from neighbouring countries.

## Horse Riding

Birthplace of the magnificent white Lipizzaner horses, **Kobilarna Lipica** (Lipica Stud Farm, Lipica 5, Sežana; tel: 05-739-1580; www.lipica.org) in the Karst region is Slovenia's top centre for horse riding. Experienced riders can take classical courses, while the less ambitious can join a group for gentle hacking. Close to Lake Bohinj, in Studor, **Mrcina Ranc** (tel: 04-531-5413; www.agencijafibula.com) is a riding centre with Icelandic ponies and Lipizzaner horses for trekking.

The top riding centre in the Soča Valley is **Pristava Lepena** (Lepena 2; tel: 05-388-9900; www.pristava-lepena.com), offering lessons and trekking on Lipizzaner horses. In addition, if you stay at a *turist kmetija* (agrotourism centre), you may well find that they have horses and ponies available.

## Sailing

Slovenia is a possible stating point for sailing down the Adriatic, although many Slovenians keep their boats in Croatia, which obviously offers much wider scope. However, there are marinas in Portorož (www.marinap.si), Izola (www.marinaizola.com) and Koper (www.marina-koper.si).

The following charter companies are based in Portorož:
**Jonathan Yachting**, Cesta solinarjev 4; tel: 05-677-8930; www.jonathan-yachting.si.
**SYS**, Cesta solinarjev 6; tel: 05-677-0119.
**Maestral**, Obala 123; tel: 05-677-9280; www.maestral.si.
Portorož Yacht Club organises a number of annual international regattas.

## Skiing

Skiing is Slovenia's favourite sport. Many Slovenians learn to ski at an early age, and Slovenia manufactures the world-renowned Elan skis (see *Shopping, page 71*). The level of the nation's skiing skills was demonstrated in 2000, when Slovenia's Davo Karničar became the first person to make an uninterrupted ski descent of the world's highest mountain, Mt Everest.

Within the country, there are many ski centres with well-maintained lifts, well-groomed pistes, snow machines, ski schools, and skiing equipment and snowboards for hire. The larger ski centres have trails for cross-country skiing, snowboarding and sledding. The season runs from December to the end of March.

In Triglav National Park is the Slovenian ski centre best known to tourists, Kranjska Gora, with more than 30km (18 miles) of groomed Alpine ski trails and over 40km (25 miles) of cross-country trails. Men's Alpine Ski World Cup events take place there each winter. Also well known is Maribor Pohorje, which hosts the annual Golden Fox competition in the women's World Cup slalom and giant slalom.

There are many other ski centres including Krvavec near Ljubljana, Rogla in the Zreče Pohorje region, Kanin towards Italy (Slovenia's highest), and Vogel near Lake Bohinj *(see page 38)*. Many of the ski centres are relatively small and attract largely local skiers.

**Above:** ready for action at Hotel Golf Glad Mokrice

## CALENDAR OF EVENTS

Most of the events listed below are connected with the Roman Catholic calendar, Slovenian folk traditions, or sporting events. All are accessible from the places featured in the itineraries.

### January/February

**New Year's Day** (1 January): The largest celebrations take place in Ljubljana, where people gather in Prešeren Square to watch a midnight fireworks display staged from the castle ramparts. Bars sell mulled wine and locals crack open bottles of champagne.

**Carnival**: Ptuj hosts *Kurentovanje*, Slovenia's biggest and most extravagant carnival, which runs from the week before the start of Lent. Inspired by ancient pagan rituals it culminates in a procession on carnival Sunday, with local men dressed as *kurenti*, clad in sheepskin cloaks, masks with long red tongues, and cowbells hung around their waists. Towns and villages throughout the country celebrate, but none can emulate Ptuj (www.ptuj-tourism.si).

**International Skiing Championships**: The slopes of Pohorje, close to Maribor, host a round of the World Cup in Women's Alpine Skiing; Planica, near Kranjska Gora hosts the Ski Jumping World Cup Championship, a three-day event attracting some 100,000 spectators; and Vitranc, also close

to Kranjska Gora, hosts the Alpine Ski World Cup, Mens' Slalom and Giant Slalom (www.slovenia.info).

### March/April

**Palm Sunday**: On the Sunday before Easter, families make or buy *butarice*, wreaths of willow and olive twigs, decorated with flowers, fruit and ribbons, and take them to church to be blessed. You can buy *butarice* at the flower stalls in the open-air market in Ljubljana the week preceding Palm Sunday.

**Easter**: On Easter Sunday families sit down to a traditional Slovenian Easter feast consisting of ham, horseradish, bread, hard-boiled eggs and *potica* (a sweet roll filled with walnuts or poppy seeds). The eggs, a symbol of fertility, are dyed and decorated with great care and are known as *pirhi*.

### May/June

Summer is celebrated with a number of Cultural Festivals (see *Nightlife*), the largest in Ljubljana, Maribor, and on the coast.

**Lace-Making Festival**: In late June **Idrija** hosts this 10-day event, combining a lace-making competition at the castle, a procession of the local miners' bands and majorettes, and displays of lace on the main square, where you can also sample the local speciality, *žlikrofi* (potato balls flavoured with marjoram, wrapped in fine dough; www.idrija-turizem.si).

**Above**: warming up for the dressage championships in Lipica

**World Championship Dressage**: A three-day programme in late May, which attracts top international riders and their horses to **Kobilarna Lipica** (Lipica Stud Farm, *see page 52*; www.lipica.org).

## July/August

In early July, **Rock Otočec** is a three-day rock festival held in the grounds of Otočec Castle in the Krka Valley.

    **Erasmus Knights' Tournament**: A one-day event at **Predjamski grad** (Predjama Castle) in the Karst region in late August, complete with jousting competitions, mounted knights in armour and ladies in period costume (www.postojna-cave.com).

## September/October

**Ex-Tempore**: For almost 40 years this international art competition has taken place in **Piran** in the first week of September. Artists are invited to work on the streets, in the squares and along the coast, and the results, selected by an international jury, are exhibited in the Town Gallery, in the Minorite Monastery cloister, and on Tartini Square (www.obalne-galerije.si).

**Glasbeni september** (Musical September): Taking place during the last two weeks of September, this festival is held in the cathedral and on Grajska trg (Castle Square) in **Maribor**, and at the Church of St George and the Festival Hall in **Ptuj**. Music ranges from classical to modern, although the event is best known for baroque performances. Workshops are also held for budding musicians (www.music-september.nd-mb.si).

**Kravji Bal** (Cows' Ball): On the shores of Lake Bohinj, at Ukanc, this rather gimmicky event (traditionally intended to celebrate the return of the cows from their mountain pastures to the valleys) features folk dancing plus plenty of eating and drinking. It takes place over a weekend in mid-September.

**Ljubljana Marathon**: An annual event since 1996, the marathon is held in late October. It is becoming increasingly popular each year, and in recent years it has attracted some 40,000 athletes from various countries (www.ljubljanskimaraton.si).

**Ceremonial Grape Harvest of the Old Vine**: A one-week festival held in **Maribor** in late September. Wine, fruit, flowers and agricultural products are on display and for sale on stalls set up around town, and concerts are performed in the Vinag Wine Cellars, on Grajska trg and in Maribor Castle. Celebrations climax when the town wine dresser harvests the Old Vine on Lent *(see page 80)*, and as the last bucket of grapes is collected a bucket of manure is delivered so that the vine can regain its growing power (www.maribor-tourism.si).

## November/December

**Martinovanje**: On St Martin's Day, 11 November, the season's 'must' (fermenting grape juice) is blessed and officially turns into wine. This is not a public holiday, but is well celebrated across the country, with a traditional feast of roast goose, accompanied by copious quantities of the wine itself.

    The largest *Martinovanje* celebrations, attracting thousands of visitors, are held on Grajski trg in **Maribor**. Various wine cellars, wine producers and taverns set up stalls offering home-made wine and food, while musical performances take place on a central stage. The festivities begin at 11.11am on 11th day of 11th month, and the wine flows freely until 8pm (www.maribor-tourism. si; www.slovenia.info).

**Christmas**: Ljubljana's castle, streets and bridges are illuminated with Christmas lights, and a Christmas Fair is held along the banks of the River Ljubljanica. Across the rest of the country, the festive season brings carol singers onto the streets and squares, and Christmas services and concerts are held in countless churches (www.visitljubljana.si).

**Living Nativity Scenes**: Between mid-December and 1 January, local schoolchildren dress up to act out nativity scenes amid stalactites and stalagmites in **Postojnska Jama** (Postojna Cave, *see page 50*) accompanied by Slovenian choirs singing Christmas carols (www.postojna-cave.com).

**Right:** organic wine on offer at Maribor's St Martin's Day celebrations

# *Practical Information*

## GETTING THERE

### By Air

Slovenia's national airline, **Adria Airways** (49 Conduit Street, London, W1S 2YS, tel: 020-7734-4630; Ljubljana, tel: 01-369 1000; www.adria.si) operates direct scheduled flights from London's Gatwick Airport (daily) and Manchester Airport (twice weekly) to Ljubljana. Flying time from London is two hours.

The low-cost airline **easyJet** (www.easyjet.com) operates daily flights from London's Stansted Airport to Ljubljana.

Ryanair (www.ryanair.com) flies between London Stansted and Trieste, just over the border in Italy.

The following airlines also fly to Slovenia and have offices in Ljubljana:

**Austrian Airlines**: tel: 04-244-3060, www.aua-si.com.

**ČSA Czech Airlines**: tel: 04-206-1750, www.czechairlines.com.

**JAT Airways**: tel: 01-231-4340, www.jat.com.

**Lufthansa**: tel: 01-239-1900, www. lufthansa.com.

**Malev Hungarian Airlines**: tel: 04-206-1676, www.malev.hu.

### By Rail

There are trains that run direct to Ljubljana from Italy, Austria, Hungary, Germany, Croatia, Serbia and Montenegro, and Macedonia. There are daily Eurocity services between Zagreb and Ljubljana (journey time 2 hours 15 minutes), Venice and Ljubljana (4 hours), Munich and Ljubljana (4 hours 30 minutes) and Vienna and Ljubljana (6 hours 15 minutes). There is also a daily Inter City service between Maribor and Graz.

### By Road

Major motorways run from the neighbouring countries of Italy, Austria, Hungary and Croatia. Residents of EU countries do not need any special insurance to enter Slovenia by car, but those from countries outside the EU require an International Green Card, which can be bought at any of the international border crossings.

**Eurolines** (www.eurolines.com) runs a comprehensive network of buses across Europe, arriving at and departing from 17 destinations in Slovenia. They operate a daily service from London (Victoria bus station) to Ljubljana (journey time 28 hours) and Maribor (journey time 31 hours), with a change in Frankfurt. In addition, numerous private companies run international services that connect Slovenia with neighbouring countries.

### By Sea

It is possible to reach Slovenia from northern Italy by boat. From March to October, the scheduled *Prince of Venice* catamaran (**Kompas**, Portorož; tel: 05-617-8000; www.kompas-online.net) runs between Venice and Izola (journey time around two hours). In addition, **Venezia Lines** (Venice, tel: 041-242-4000; www.venezialines.com) run regular summer catamarans from Venice to Piran (journey time two hours 15 minutes).

**Left:** World Trade Centre, Ljubljana
**Right:** making the trains run on time

## TRAVEL ESSENTIALS

### Visas & Passports

A passport is generally required to enter Slovenia, though EU and Swiss citizens need just an identity card for stays of up to 30 days. Slovenia is a Schengen Agreement country, so there are few controls at the Austrian and Italian borders. Visitors from the

US, Canada, Australia and New Zealand have their passports stamped upon entry and exit, but do not require visas for stays of up to three months. Visitors from other countries should check with Slovenian consulates. There is also information at www.slovenia.info and www.mzz.gov.si.

### Customs

Now that Slovenia is in the EU, you do not have to pay any tax or duty on goods such as alcohol and cigarettes that you have bought tax-paid in other EU countries, so long as they are for your own personal use. If you are arriving direct from a non-EU country, you can bring in duty-free a maximum of 1 litre of spirits, 2 litres of wine and 200 cigarettes (or 50 cigars).

### Climate and When to Go

Although Slovenia is a small country, dramatic differences in topography mean that the climate varies greatly from region to region. The northwest has an Alpine climate, and temperatures in the Alpine valleys are moderate in summer but cold in winter. The Adriatic coast and the Karst area have a Mediterranean climate, with hot summers and mild winters. Most of eastern Slovenia has a continental climate, with hot summers and cold winters. January is the coldest month with an average national daytime temperature of -2°C (28°F) while July is the warmest with an average of 21°C (70°F).

There are two separate tourist seasons in Slovenia: summer (late May to early Oct) when it is warm enough to swim, and winter (mid-Dec to late Mar) when there is excellent snow for skiing. To avoid the crowds, visit in spring or autumn.

### Electricity

The electric supply is 220V, 50Hz. Most plugs have two round pins in the common European format: pack an adaptor for appliances you bring from home. US visitors need a voltage transformer, except for such electronic equipment as laptop computers, which usually have dual voltage.

### Time Differences

Slovenia is one hour ahead of GMT and adopts daylight savings time in summer.

## GETTING ACQUAINTED

### Geography

Slovenia is a small green country, similar in size to Wales or Israel. It is predominantly hilly, with more than 90 percent of its surface over 300m (984ft) above sea level, and several mountains rising above 2,500m (8,200ft). Almost half of the country is covered by woodland, with agricultural land covering a further 43 percent. There are six main regions: the Alps, the pre-Alpine hills, the Dinaric Karst, the 47-km (29-mile) coastal strip, the flat Pannonian plain and the lowlands.

### Government & Economy

Since Slovenia gained independence in 1991 the political scene has been dominated by the centre-left Social Democrats. However, in 2004 a centre-right coalition gained

**Above:** Sunday morning get-together

*practical information*

power, only to lose it again in the 2008 elections to a centre-left coalition formed by prime minister Borut Pahor of the Social Democrats. The president is former UN diplomat Danilo Turk.

When Slovenia joined the EU in May 2004, it had the healthiest economy of all the new member countries. With a GDP per capita income of US$12,000 a year, Slovenians were earning twice as much as the accession country average and 70 percent of the EU average. In fact, the economy has been doing so well that in January 2004 the International Monetary Fund (IMF) officially recognised Slovenia as 'emerged' and in March 2004 Slovenia became the first Central European transition country to be promoted from borrower status to donor partner at the World Bank. In 2007 it also became the first of the new EU member countries to adopt the euro. About 25 percent of industry remains under state control – privatisation is taking place slowly and cautiously. In 2008 Slovenia held the EU presidency.

## Population

The majority of the population – 83 percent – is Slovenian, with minority groups of Italians and Hungarians (both are guaranteed two seats in Parliament), plus people from the other republics of the former Yugoslavia (who declare themselves as Serbs, Croats, Yugoslavs, Muslims, or Macedonians).

## Religion

The predominant religion in the country is Roman Catholic (72 percent), followed by 4.3 percent who declare themselves as atheist, 2.4 percent Eastern Orthodox, 1 percent Muslim and 1 percent Protestant.

## MONEY MATTERS

### Currency

On 1 January 2007, Slovenia was the first of the new EU member countries to adopt the euro (€), which replaced the tolar.

### Credit Cards

Most hotels, restaurants and shops accept the major credit cards: American Express, Diner's Club, Mastercard and Visa.

### Cash Machines

Most banks, even those in small provincial towns, have cash machines (ATMs).

### Tipping

A service charge is not included in restaurant bills. If you have enjoyed your meal and are satisfied with the service, it is normal to add on 10 percent.

## GETTING AROUND

### To and From the Airport

Ljubljana Airport (tel: 04-206-1000; www.lju-airport.si) is located at Brnik, 23km (14 miles) from the city centre. From Monday to Friday there is an hourly bus service between the airport and the capital; on Saturday and Sunday this is reduced to a two-hourly service. Tickets are sold on the bus, and the journey takes approximately 45 minutes, depending on traffic. Taxis are available in front of the terminal building – expect to pay about €40 to the city centre.

### Taxi

Taxi services operate in all the larger towns and tourist resorts, and drivers are obliged to run a meter.

### Train

Travelling by train *(vlak)* is more comfortable and slightly cheaper than travelling by bus, but due to Slovenia's mountainous terrain the railway network is limited. However, **Slovenske železnice** (Slovenian Railways; tel: 01-291-3332; www.slo-zeleznice.si) run regular and efficient services between major towns, including Ljubljana to Maribor (about 30 trains daily, Intercity 1 hour 45 minutes, local trains 2 hours 15 minutes); Maribor to Ptuj (about

**Right:** meet the locals

12 trains daily, journey time 50 minutes) and Ljubljana to Koper (seven trains daily, journey time 2 hours 20 minutes).

Note that neither Lake Bled nor Lake Bohinj have railway stations. The resort of Bled on the shores of Lake Bled is served by

Lesce-Bled station, which lies about 4km (2 ½ miles) from the lake, while Ribčev Laz, overlooking Lake Bohinj, is served by Bohinjska Bistrica which is even more of a hike, at 6km (4 miles).

From late June to early September, two vintage steam locomotives run along scenic routes in the northwest of the country. One operates along the Bohinj line, running Jesenice–Bled–Bohinj–Most na Soči, offering views of Lake Bled and the stunning mountains and valleys of Triglav National Park (for details contact **ABC Rent-a-car**, Ljubljana; tel: 01-510-4320; www.europcar.si) while the other service covers a stretch of the Transalpina Railway running from the Italian border into Slovenia Gorizia–Nova Gorica–Most na Soči-Bled, following the Soča Valley and crossing a series of tunnels, bridges and viaducts (for details contact **Club** tourist agency, Most na Soči; tel: 05-381-3050; www.club.si).

### Bus

The bus *(avtobus)* network is considerably more extensive than the railways, so for most small out-of-the-way destinations it is the only public transport option. In fact, you can get to even the most remote areas of the country by bus, although the journey may take some time and involve several changes. They do, however, allow you to see a lot of the countryside. For further information on national buses, contact Ljubljana Bus Station (tel: 01-234-4600; www.ap-ljubljana.si).

### Car

Since 1994 a national motorway *(avtocesta)* construction programme has been underway, envisaging the building of motorway links in two directions: northeast–southwest from Šentilj to Koper (also branching off to the Hungarian and Italian borders); and northwest–southeast from the Karavanke Tunnel on the Austrian border to Obrežje on the Croatian border. The two routes will intersect at the Ljubljana ring road. If building progress runs to plan the entire project should be finished by 2013.

To drive on most sections of Slovenian motorway you must buy a vignette *(vinjeta)* for a week, a month or a year (currently €15, €30 and €95) and stick it inside your windscreen. These are available in many places including petrol stations, supermarkets, post offices and travel agencies, and are often on sale at petrol stations outside Slovenia, near the border. For further details see www.dars.si.

When driving in Slovenia, remember that you must have your headlights switched on at all times, even during daylight hours. On main roads most petrol stations are open 24 hours. The police *(policija)* are ever on the alert for speeding motorists. Speed limits are: 50km/h (31mph) in built-up areas; 90km/h (56mph) on local roads; 100km/h (62mph) on highways; and 130km/h (81mph) on motorways.

Drinking and driving can lead to severe fines and the confiscation of your licence – the maximum legal blood-alcohol level is 0.5g/kg. Note that many mountain roads, such as the Vršič Pass, are closed during winter due to snow.

**Avto moto zveza Slovenije** (Automobile Association of Slovenia, AMZS) provides 24-hour assistance for problems on the road (tel: 1987; www. amzs.si).

There are car-hire companies in all main towns as well as in tourist resorts and at Ljubljana airport.

**Above:** Slovenia's trains are comfortable and efficient

## HOURS & HOLIDAYS

### Business Hours

Banks, post offices and most shops close on public holidays. Most **banks** are open Monday to Friday 8.30am–12.30pm and 2–5pm, Saturday 8.30am–noon. Most **post offices** are open Monday to Friday 8am–6pm, Saturday 8am–noon. **Shops** are generally open Monday–Friday 8am–7pm, Saturday 8am–1pm. The majority are closed on Sunday, although some private establishments now remain open. **Museums** are usually open Tuesday–Sunday 10am–6pm throughout the summer, with reduced winter hours.

### Public Holidays

New Year's Day – 1 and 2 January
Prešeren Day – 8 February
Easter Sunday and Monday – variable
Day of Uprising against Occupation – 27 April
May Day – 1 and 2 May
Slovenia Day – 25 June
Assumption Day – 15 August
Reformation Day – 31 October
All Saints' Day – 1 November
Christmas Day – 25 December
Independence Day – 26 December

### Market Days

All the larger towns have a market from Monday–Saturday, from 7am–2pm. In the smaller towns a market may take place once or twice a week.

## ACCOMMODATION

Hotels range from stately old villas and castles that have been converted to provide luxury accommodation, to 1970s concrete, socialist-style complexes, which may lack character but invariably have excellent recreational facilities. If you are travelling on a budget there are a number of options. Try youth hostels (you will find one of the most outstanding in Europe in Ljubljana), or there's private accommodation, which can be booked through local tourist offices and travel agencies; and there are campsites – among the best are those at Zlatorog by Lake Bohinj and at Fiesa near Piran. Alternatively, to get a real taste of rural life, stay at a *turist kmetija* (agrotourism centre; www.slovenia.info/touristfarms).

Along the coast, prices go up during high season (July–Aug), when hotels and hostels may be fully booked in advance. In Ljubljana, prices are constant throughout the year, although there may be a dearth of rooms during international trade fairs. Some places add a 30 percent surcharge for stays of less than three days.

Prices are posted in euros (€). The following price codes are based on two people sharing a double room in peak season, with breakfast:

| | |
|---|---|
| € | up to €60 |
| €€ | €60–120 |
| €€€ | €120–180 |
| €€€€ | over €180 |

### Ljubljana

**Celica Youth Hostel**
*Metelkova 8*
*Tel: 01-230-9700*
*www.souhostel.com*
Originally built in the 19th century as a prison, this hostel has to be one of the most remarkable youth hostels in Europe. The former cells have been individually redesigned by artists and architects to provide 20 two-bed rooms on the first floor,

**Right:** the impressive façade of the Grand Hotel Union, Ljubljana

plus dormitories on the floors above. Facilities include a café, exhibition space, Internet corner and a meditation room. It's so special they offer guided tours daily at 2pm. Close to railway and bus stations, too. Reservations essential. €

### City Hotel
*Dalmatinova 15*
*Tel: 01-239-0000*
*www.cityhotel.si*
Close to bus and railway stations, this mid-range hotel was recently renovated to provide 123 comfortable rooms. Facilities include Internet corner and bike hire. €€

### Domina Grand Media Hotel
*Dunajska 160*
*Tel: 01-588-2500*
*www.dominahotels.it*
Close to the trade exhibition centre, 3km (2 miles) north of the railway station, this hotel opened in 2004 and claims to be one of the most technologically advanced and funkiest designer hotels in the world. There are 214 rooms and 120 suites, a fitness centre, beauty centre, and casino. €€€

### Grand Hotel Union
*Miklošičeva 1–3*
*Tel: 01-308-1170*
*www.gh-union.si*
Housed in an impressive white Secessionist-style building from 1905, this hotel has 172 sumptuous rooms, 6 suites and 16 apartments. Facilities include a pool on the top floor, with views over the city, a fitness centre, sauna and massage. It's located in the

centre of town, between the railway station and the river. €€€€

### Hotel Emonec
*Wolfova 12*
*Tel: 01-200-1520*
*www.hotel-emonec.com*
The best low-cost hotel in town, the Emonec is centrally located between Kongresni trg and Presernov trg. It has 26 modern, comfortable rooms with en-suite bathrooms, plus an internet corner and bicycles for hire. €€

## Krka Valley
### Hotel Grad Otočec
*Grajska 2, Otočec 5*
*Tel: 07-384-8900*
*www.terme-krka.si*
Lying on an island on the River Krka, accessed via a wooden bridge, this 13th-century Gothic-Renaissance castle, complete with four towers, has been refurbished to become a luxury hotel, with 14 rooms and 2 suites. All the furniture is antique and staff dress in period costume. You'll find it 8km (5 miles) west of Šentjernej, on the road to Novo Mesto. €€€€

### Šeruga
*Sela pri Ratežu 15, Otočec*
*Tel: 07-334-6900*
*www.seruga.si*
Complete with traditional-style old farm buildings, this friendly agrotourism centre lies 10km (6 miles) from Novo Mesto and 4km (2.5 miles) from Otočec Castle. Best known for its excellent home cooking, it has nine double rooms and one apartment, each with traditional wooden furniture. Guests are welcome to join in farm activities. €

## Lake Bled
### Bledec Youth Hostel
*Grajska 17*
*Tel: 04-574-5250*
*www.youth-hostel-bledec.si*
Situated on the hill above the lake, on the way to the castle, this youth hostel offers excellent value for money. The 13 rooms, which all have wooden floors and dark wood furniture, have a total of 55 beds. The

**Above:** the Grand Hotel Toplice has a terrific view of Lake Bled

facilities include a restaurant with an open-air terrace, and a common room with Internet facilities. €

### Grand Hotel Toplice
*Cesta svobode 20*
*Tel: 04-579-1000*
*www.hotel-toplice.com*
The very height of fashion when it first opened in 1875, this hotel was extended in 1931 and fully renovated in 2002. The 54 rooms and 33 suites, all with balconies, are individually furnished in classical style. Facilities include an indoor pool filled with thermal waters, massage and sauna. Top quality but expensive. €€€€

### Vila Bled
*Cesta svobode 26*
*Tel: 04-579-1500*
*www.vila-bled.com*
This was Tito's former summer villa, set in 5 hectares (12 acres) of gardens, with a sweeping flight of steps running down to Lake Bled. It has been converted into a luxury hotel with 10 rooms and 20 apartments, all with 1950s decor. Guests have free use of the recreational facilities at the Grand Hotel Toplice *(see above)*. €€€

## Bohinj

### Bellevue
*Ribčev laz 65*
*Tel: 04-572-3331*
*www.hoteli-bohinj.si*
This is where Agatha Christie stayed while writing *Murder on the Orient Express* (Room 206) and it remains comfortable and restful, with an appropriately old-fashioned, somewhat shabby appearance. It's located amid pine woods on a hill above Lake Bohinj, and its upstairs rooms offer great views over the surrounding landscape. The 50 rooms all have TV and telephone, and most have balconies. €€

### Jezero
*Ribčev laz 51*
*Tel: 04-572-3375*
*www.bohinj.si*
This modern, Alpine-style hotel lies at the east end of the lake, next to the Tourist Information Centre and the bus stop. There are 63

pleasant rooms and three suites, most of which have balconies. Facilities include an indoor pool, sauna, massage, gymnasium and an Internet corner. €€

## Soča Valley

### Hvala
*Trg Svobode 1, Kobarid*
*Tel: 05-389-9300*
*www.topli-val-sp.si*
This friendly, family-run hotel overlooking Kobarid's main square has 31 rooms, with sleek minimalist Italian furniture, en-suite bathroom, hairdryer, satellite TV and telephone. Service is professional and helpful and the Topli Val restaurant (see *Eating Out*) on the ground floor is outstanding. €€

## Piran, Portorož and Secovlje

### Barbara Fiesa
*Fiesa 68, Piran*
*Tel: 05-617-9000*
*www.hotelbarbarafiesa.com*
A 15-minute walk along the seafront from the old town will bring you to this friendly waterfront hotel. Renovated in 2006, it now has 36 double rooms and six family rooms, each with a sea view and balcony. There is a pebble beach at the front, plus a swimming pool, a gym and a sauna on the ground floor. €€

### Grand Hotel Portorož
*Obala 43, Portorož*
*Tel: 05-692-9001*
*www.lifeclass.net*
A modern hotel and spa right on the seafront promenade, with 185 double rooms and 13 suites, plus a pool, a fitness centre and a spa offering various massage and hydro-massage treatments. Rooms with a sea view cost a just a little more. €€€

### Tartini
*Tartinijev trg 15, Piran*
*Tel: 05-671-1000*
*www.hotel-tartini-piran.com*
In an idyllic location overlooking Piran's delightful main square, the Tartini has 43 rooms – the best have balconies overlooking the square or the harbour – plus a rooftop terrace with a small pool. €€

**Val Hostel**
*Gregorčičeva 38a, Piran*
*Tel: 05-673-2555*
*www.hostel-val.com*
Hidden away in the old town, this hostel has 56 beds divided between 22 rooms, with shared bathrooms on each floor. Facilities include use of the kitchen, laundry, restaurant, TV and Internet corner. €

### Idrija and Nova Gorica

**Kendov dvorec**
*Spodnja Idrija, 4km (2½ miles) from Idrija*
*Tel: 05-372-5100*
*www.kendov-dvorec.com*
This attractive 14th-century manor house has been carefully restored and converted into a fine luxury hotel with 11 individually furnished rooms, filled with antiques. Many rate it among Slovenia's top hotels – the rich and famous come here for wedding receptions and honeymoons. €€€

**Perla**
*Kidričeva 7, Nova Gorica*
*Tel: 05-336-3000*
*www.hit.si*
Claiming to be one of the largest entertainment centres in Europe, the Perla was extended in 2006 and now has 273 rooms and 19 suites. Facilities include the 24-hour casino (roulette, blackjack, poker, slot machines), a beauty and fitness centre with a pool and sauna, as well as a nightclub with guest performers. €€€

### Koper

**Hotel Koper**
*Pristaniška 3, Koper*
*Tel: 05-610-0500*
*www.terme-catez.si*
Located on the edge of the old town, overlooking the sea, this 1970s hotel has 55 rooms and 10 suites, most with balconies and sea views, and all with en-suite bathrooms, satellite TV and mini-bar. Guests have free use of the indoor and outdoor pools at the nearby sister hotel, the Aquapark Hotel Žusterna. €€

### Maribor

**Orel**
*Grajski trg 3a*
*Tel: 02-250-6700*
*www.termemb.si*
Lying in the heart of the old town, this is Maribor's most central hotel. It was renovated in 2006 and has 80 modern, comfortable rooms, each with en-suite bathroom, cable TV, telephone and mini-bar. €€€

**Piramida**
*Ulica Heroja Šlandra 10*
*Tel: 02-234-4400*
*www.termemb.si*
Between the old town and the railway and bus stations, this six-storey hotel has been refurbished to provide 70 well-equipped guest rooms. Functional rather than atmospheric, it is well geared to business travellers, and has a business club and a mini relaxation centre. €€€

### Ptuj and the Jeruzalem Wine Road

**Garni Hotel Mitra**
*Prešernova ulica 6, Ptuj*
*Tel: 02-787-7455*
*www.hotel-mitra.si*
Easy to spot, thanks to its pink façade, this refurbished hotel, dating back to 1870, lies in the heart of the old town, just off Slovenski trg. It has 23 smart guest rooms, each with reproduction furniture. €€€

**Above:** family-friendly farm accommodation

**Hlebec**
*Kog 108, Kog*
*Tel: 02-713-7060*
This is a family run wine-cellar that serves food as well as offering overnight accommodation. The seven double rooms all have hand-made wooden furniture, which is not lacquered but treated with beeswax, giving off a distinctive smell of honey. Each room has a television and an en-suite bathroom, and some of them have balconies. €

**Ptuj Youth Hostel**
*Osojnikova 9, Ptuj*
*Tel: 02-771-0814*
Close to the bus and railway stations, this youth hostel has 13 rooms, all with modern furnishings, and a total of 69 beds. Meals are available on request. €

**Taverna**
*Svetinje 21, Ivanjkovci*
*Tel: 02-719-4128*
*www.taverna-jeruzalem.si*
Located on a hilltop with views over the surrounding vineyards, this is first and foremost a restaurant and wine cellar. However, they also have 11 simple but very comfortable double rooms for guests upstairs. Advance reservations essential. €

## Rogaška Slatina

**Grand hotel Sava and Hotel Zagreb**
*Zdravlišči trg 6*
*Tel: 03-811-4000*
*www.hotel-sava-rogaska.si*
These two interconnected hotels have a total of 207 single rooms, 116 doubles and 20 suites, all with en-suite bathroom and satellite TV. Facilities include the luxurious Lotus Wellness Centre and Spa *(see page 67)*, plus a restaurant catering for special diets. €€€

**Hotel Strossmayer**
*Zdravlišči trg 14*
*Tel: 03-811-2000*
*www.terme-rogaska.si*
Built in 1848, this historic place was Rogaška's most exclusive hotel during the 19th century, when the Austro–Hungarian Emperor Franz Jozef I used to stay here. It was completely renovated in 2003, to provide 72 rooms and three suites. €€

# HEALTH & EMERGENCIES

## Medical Treatment
All foreign visitors have the right to emergency medical care. Upon the presentation of a valid European Health Insurance Card (EHIC), all EU member-country passport holders are entitled to free medical attention in public health institutions and from private doctors who have made an agreement with the Health Insurance Institute if Slovenia (HIIS). (UK citizens can obtain the EHIC application form from any main post office, by phone, tel: 0845 605 0707, or on-line at www.ehic.org.uk.) Visitors from countries that do not have a reciprocal agreement with Slovenia are required to pay for medical treatment; they are strongly advised to take out private travel insurance (covering medical emergencies) before leaving home.

## Emergency Telephone Numbers
**Police**: 113
**Fire**: 112
**Ambulance**: 112
**Road Assistance**: 1987

## Pharmacies
Pharmacies are generally open Monday–Friday 7am–7pm and Saturday 8am–1pm. In larger towns you will find at least one pharmacy open on Sunday and throughout the night for emergencies. The following are on duty 24 hours:
**Ljubljana**: Prisojna ulica 7; tel: 01-230-6230.
**Maribor**: Lekarna Glavni trg, Glavni trg 20; tel: 02-229-4740.

## Security and Crime
Slovenia is safer than most West European countries, but you should always take sensible precautions with personal possessions.

**Right:** a familiar name in Koper

## COMMUNICATIONS & POST

### Post

Airmail letters and postcards take from three to five days to reach other European countries, seven to 10 days to the US and Canada, and 10 to 14 days to Australia. You can buy *znamke* (stamps) at any *pošta* (post office), a building easily identified by its yellow sign.

### Telephone

Direct international calls can be made from public phone booths in the street if you have a *telefonska kartica* (phone card), available from post offices and newspaper kiosks. For more privacy, call from a cabin at the post office – the one on Trg OF by the railway station in Ljubljana is open 24 hours. Calls are cheaper between 7pm and 7am.

Dial 00 to call abroad, followed by the country code (UK: 44; Canada and US: 1 Australia: 61) then the area code and number you wish to reach. To call Slovenia from abroad, dial 386, then omit the first 0.

**International directory enquiries**: 989
**Local directory enquiries**: 988

## MEDIA

### Newspapers

A wide selection of foreign-language newspapers and magazine is available in Ljubljana all year round, and in tourist resorts during the peak seasons.

### Television

Most hotels have satellite TV in the guest rooms, programmed to pick up English, Italian, German and Croatian channels. Films are normally shown in the original version with Slovenian sub-titles, so it's worth checking out the Slovenian channels for these.

### Radio

Radio Slovenija International is a 24-hour station that broadcasts in Slovenian, German and English, offering a good mix of international music and news stories. You can pick it up at 102.4MHz in the Ljubljana area, 98.9 MHz along the coast and 102.8 MHz in the northeast close to Maribor.

## USEFUL INFORMATION

### Maps

The Slovenian Tourist Board publishes an excellent map of the country, which is provided free to visitors. Most local Tourist Information Centres offer free plans of the towns they represent or, if they are in rural areas, maps of hiking routes in the surrounding countryside.

### Bookshops

The largest publishing houses are **Mladinska Knjiga** and **Cankarjeva Založba**, both of which have bookshops in Ljubljana, Maribor and Koper, stocking a limited selection of imported English-language guide books, fiction and non-fiction.

### Language

The official language is Slovenian, a grammatically complex South Slavic tongue written in Latin script. The country's Hungarian and Italian minorities speak their own languages. Fortunately for visitors, the younger generation of Slovenians usually speak good English plus either Italian or German.

## USEFUL ADDRESSES

### Tourist Information Centres

**Slovenian Tourist Board**: Dunjaska 156 Ljubljana; tel: 01-589-1840; www.slovenia info.

**Bled**: Cesta svobode 10, Bled; tel: 04-574-1122; www.bled.si.

**Above:** you will come across some signs in English – especially in relation to tourism

*practical information*

**Bohinj**: Ribčev Laz 48, Bohinjsko Jezero; tel: 04-574-6010; www.bohinj.si.

**Idrija**: Vodnikova 3; tel: 05-374-3916; www.idrija.si.

**Koper**: Titov trg 3, Koper; tel: 05-664-6403; www.koper.si.

**Lipica Stud Farm**: Lipica 5, Sežana; tel: 05-739-1580; www.lipica.org.

**Ljubljana City**: Krekov trg 10; tel: 01-306-1215; www.visitljubljana.si.

**Ljutomer**: Jureša Cirila 4, Ljutomer; tel: 02-584-8333; www.prlekija.si.

**Maribor**: Partizanska cesta 47, Maribor; tel: 02-234-6611; www.maribor-pohorje.si.

**Nova Gorica**: Bevkov trg 4; tel: 05-330-4600; www.novagorica-turizem.com.

**Piran**: Tartinijev trg 2, Pian; tel: 05-673-4440; www.portoroz.si.

**Portorož**: Obala 16, Portorož; tel: 05-674-2220; www.portoroz.si.

**Postojnska Jama**: Jamska cesta 9, Postojna; tel: 05-720-1610; www.postojna-cave.com.

**Ptuj**: Slovenska cesta 3; tel: 02-779-6011; www.ptuj-tourism.si.

**Štanjel**: Štanjel 42; tel: 05-769-0056; www.kras-carso.com.

## Information Offices Abroad

**UK**: South Marlands, Itchingfield, Horsham, West Sussex, RH13 0NN; tel: 0870-225-5305.

**US**: 345 East 12th Street, New York, NY 10003; tel: 212-358-9686.

## Embassies & Consulates

**Australian Consulate**: Trg republike 3/XII; tel: 01-425-4252.

**Bristish Embassy**: Trg republike 3/IV; tel: 01-200-3910.

**Canadian Consulate**: Miklošičeva 19; tel: 01-252-4444.

**US Embassy**: Prešernova 31; tel: 01-200-5500.

## FURTHER READING

*The Death of Yugoslavia* by Laura Silber and Allan Little (Penguin Group and BBC Worldwide Ltd, London, 1996). Based on the BBC documentary of the same name, this book traces the events that led to the eventual break-up of Yugoslavia, with individual chapters dedicated to the Slovenian Spring of 1988 and Slovenia's 10-day fight for independence in 1991, plus the tragic wars that followed in Croatia and Bosnia.

*Slovenia and the Slovenes: A Small State and the New Europe* by Catherine Carmichael and James Gow (Indiana University Press, 2001). Traces the development of the Slovenian national identity and the political, economic, military and cultural life of its people through the ages.

*Independent Slovenia: Origins, Movements, Prospects* by Jill Benderly (Palgrave Macmillan, 1996). Essays examining the historical, cultural, political and economic origins of the drive for independence, as well as the country's future prospects.

*A Farewell to Arms* by Ernest Hemingway (Scribner, reprinted 1992). Inspired by Hemingway's own experiences in World War I, this is the story of an American ambulance driver and a British nurse who meet in Italy during the war and fall in love. A story of passion and pain, loyalty and desertion, it gives a detailed account of the fighting that took place around Kobarid (referred to here by its Italian name, Caporetto).

*Walking in the Julian Alps* by Simon Brown (Cicerone Press, 1993). Dividing the northwest region into four areas (Bled, Bohinj, Kranjska Gora and Bovec) this handbook lays out a series of walks, ranging from easy to difficult, with clear and accurate route descriptions, as well as giving the reader some idea of the countryside and views they will encounter en route.

**Right:** a corner of Izola where time seems to stand still
**Following pages:** picturesque Škofja Loka, in the northwest of the country

## ACKNOWLEDGEMENTS

| | |
|---|---|
| *All photography by* | **Gregory Wrona/Apa** |
| | **and Neil Buchan-Grant/APA** |
| *Additional Photography* | |
| *10* | **Slovenian Government Public** |
| | **Relations and Media Office** |
| *14* | **Bettmann/Corbis** |
| *12* | **Stefano Blanchetti/Corbis** |
| *15* | **S.I.N./Corbis** |
| *11, 13* | **TopFoto.co.uk** |
| *Front cover* | **4Corners Images/Johanna Huber** |
| *Back cover* | **Gregory Wrona/Apa** |

© APA Publications GmbH & Co. Verlag KG Singapore Branch, Singapore

## INDEX

credits & index